MEDIEVAL
COMBAT

Hans Talhoffer

Hans Talhoffer

MEDIEVAL COMBAT

A Fifteenth-Century Illustrated Manual of
Swordfighting and Close-Quarter Combat

Translated and Edited by Mark Rector
Foreword by John Clements

Greenhill Books, London
Stackpole Books, Pennsylvania

Medieval Combat: A Fifteenth-Century Illustrated Manual of Swordfighting and Close-Quarter Combat first published 2000 by Greenhill Books, Lionel Leventhal Limited, Park House, 1 Russell Gardens, London NW11 9NN and Stackpole Books, 5067 Ritter Road, Mechanicsburg, PA 17055, USA

British Library Cataloguing in Publication Data
Talhoffer, Hans
Medieval combat : a fifteenth-century illustrated manual of
swordfighting and close-quarter combat
1.Swordplay - History 2.Fencing - History
3.Military art and science - History - Medieval, 500-1500 4.Combat - History
I.Title
355.4'0902
ISBN 1-85367-418-4

Library of Congress Cataloging-in-Publication Data
Talhoffer, Hans, ca. 1420-ca. 1490.
[Fechtbuch, aus dem Jahre 1467. English]
Medieval combat : a fifteenth-century illustrated manual of swordfighting and
close-quarter combat / Hans Talhoffer ; translated and edited by Mark Rector.
p.   cm.
Includes bibliographical references.
ISBN 1-85367-418-4
1. Fencing—Europe—Early works to 1800. 2. Hand-to-hand fighting—Europe—Early
works to 1800. I. Rector, Mark. II. Title.
U860.T14 2000
355.5'47—dc21   00-037194

Printed and bound in Great Britain by Creative Print and Design (Wales), Ebbw Vale

CONTENTS

FOREWORD

A Modern Renaissance in Medieval Martial Arts

Today the term 'martial arts' is usually assumed to be synonymous with 'Asian fighting art'. This is no surprise since popular media are notorious for misrepresenting medieval fighting. The medieval warrior's craft is often reduced to the myth that combatants merely crudely bludgeoned one another or hacked and slashed savagely. Yet well established, highly sophisticated European fighting systems existed. European 'masters of defence' produced hundreds of detailed, well–illustrated technical manuals on their fighting methods, and the people of the Germanic states were especially prolific. Their manuals present to us a portrait of highly developed and innovative European martial arts based on sophisticated, systematic and effective skills. Among the best known of these works is that of Hans Talhoffer. His influential treatise, first produced in 1443, was reproduced many times throughout the century.

Here now is the first English-language edition of the definitive work of this *Fechtmeister* (literally, 'fight master'). Talhoffer, probably a follower of the Grand *Fechtmeister* Hans Liechtenauer, reveals an array of great-sword and two-handed sword techniques, sword and buckler moves, dagger fighting, seizures and disarms, grappling techniques, and the Austrian wrestling of Ott, a rare medieval Jewish master of whom little is known. The illustrated plates also show methods for judicial duels – official fights to end legal disputes – and fighting with pole-weapons. Like many other medieval fighting texts, Talhoffer's manual covers fighting in full armour and without armour.

His manual reveals a range of both rudimentary and advanced techniques and provides a firm foundation on which to begin exploration of Western martial culture and the skills of medieval masters of defence. His manual covers fighting with swords, shields, spears, staffs, pole-axes and daggers, as well as grappling, throws, takedowns, holds and ground-fighting skills. Like many other teachers of his day, Talhoffer recognized that armed and unarmed fighting were only facets of personal combat and he accordingly taught an integrated art. He was greatly concerned with secrecy in both the teaching and learning of his skills, for if a fighter's style were known he could be vulnerable, and a master's teaching was his own to give out as he saw fit. Talhoffer's manual was not widely distributed until after his death, and even then it must have circulated very slowly among groups of practitioners.

Whether your interest is academic, historical, theatrical or martial, Talhoffer's work offers today's student of European martial culture a strong starting point. While not a complete guide book on fighting from the period, it will encourage the reader's own practice and understanding of the brutal effectiveness of European warriors as well as the artistry of their craft. Like many others, for years now I have been interpreting and practising Talhoffer's techniques. I have studied his instructions and followed his advice with real weapons and with safe sparring tools. It has been a long but fruitful process and while such investigation remains ongoing and new insights continually appear, there is no question of the martial value and legitimacy of his teachings.

It is exciting that we are currently seeing a 'renaissance' in the study of Western martial culture as research and study of historical European fighting arts now undergoes something of a revival. Increasingly, enthusiasts of historical fencing today are focusing on legitimate methods rather than mere competitive games and role-playing pursuits and a much greater appreciation for the sophistication and effectiveness of medieval and Renaissance fighting skills has emerged. A new generation of serious practitioners and researchers is approaching the subject not as escapist fantasy or entertainment, not just as theatrical display, but as the study of a true martial art.

Earnest practice of the methods of medieval and Renaissance weaponry is increasing in popularity today as students rediscover the many works of European masters of defence. A renewed interest in and appreciation of the formidability and complexity of both medieval and Renaissance arms and armour has evolved. Most satisfying is the tremendous increase in the availability of translations of the old fighting manuals, but even so we have only begun to scratch the surface in the serious study of medieval fighting arts. Talhoffer's *Fechtbuch* ('fight book') represents the tip of a very large iceberg.

John Clements
Author of *Medieval Swordsmanship* and
Director of the Historical Armed Combat Association
2000

INTRODUCTION

This is the very first English translation of Master Hans Talhoffer's *Fechtbuch*, or 'Fight Book', from the year 1467, one of the most influential and lavishly drawn fencing manuals of the fifteenth century. Talhoffer (*c*1420–*c*1490) was master of arms to the Swabian knight Leutold von Königsegg, a feudatory of Count Eberhardt the Bearded of Württemberg.[1] At least six illustrated manuals were produced under Talhoffer's name, covering an astonishing variety of armed and unarmed combat techniques. The most commonly known manuscripts were drawn in 1443, 1459 and 1467. Fencing scholar Gustav Hergsell discovered this last manual at the end of the nineteenth century in the library of Ernst II, Duke of Saxe-Coburg-Gotha, and translated the original Swabian text into German, publishing his version in Prague in 1887.

Hergsell describes Talhoffer's manuscript in his introduction:

> The original drawings were made with pen and ink on parchment sheets, and boldly coloured. The cross is drawn in red upon the shields, caps, chests and backs of the shield-fighters. In some of the drawings, blood spurts from wounds, and the shields are coloured yellow. The drawings appear on both sides of each leaf.
>
> The captions ... are inscribed in a bold hand. They alone set out the particular fights, as this codex contains neither a title nor any other text.
>
> Next to the final illustration, showing a fight on horseback with crossbow and spear (jousting lance), Talhoffer himself is depicted, sword in hand, with the inscription, 'This book was written by Hans Talhoffer, who posed for this portrait.'[2]

As Hergsell notes, this book contains no explanatory text beyond the captions to the illustrations, and these are often oblique and open to multiple interpretations. The illustrations themselves are not always arranged to form coherent sequences. Personal combat training was a highly competitive field in medieval Europe, and fencing masters zealously guarded the secrets of their craft. Talhoffer's manuscript is often intentionally arcane. Yet it was not written as a fencing treatise, nor, strictly speaking, a 'how to' book. Rather, Talhoffer meant it as a declaration of his ability as a master of arms, and as a professional field manual for the practical application of killing techniques with the prescribed weapons. A certain amount of martial knowledge and skill is assumed of the reader, and many things are left unsaid. However, with a little effort, the mists obscuring the master's teachings may be blown clear and his true meaning revealed. The captions to the plates are freely, rather than literally, translated from the original Swabian (which can be found in the Appendix to this book), and expanded in some cases. Additional explanatory information can be found in the translator's notes. While I have endeavoured in my translation to remain true to the original text, I have taken care to make the captions understandable to the modern reader, without resorting to too much modern or medieval fencing jargon.

Two plates in Talhoffer's *Fechtbuch* are not included: 127 (an almost blank leaf, with barely distinguishable outlines showing a shield fight in all openings), and 222 (a blank leaf).

The individual sections in Talhoffer's book may be divided into two sorts: those dealing with the 'judicial duel' and those concerned with personal combat. The judicial duel was an officially sanctioned fight to resolve a legal dispute, and was common in Western Europe from the tenth through the fifteenth century.[3] Talhoffer illustrates noblemen fighting a trial by combat in full armour with the sword and the spear. For commoners, the judicial duel involved unique and occasionally bizarre weapon combinations and ritual costumes: the combatants were stitched into cowled leather suits, greased with pig fat, and armed with a selection of wooden maces, swords, and spiked and hooked shields. These trials were rarely 'first blood' affairs, but duels to the death.

One of the most curious episodes Talhoffer illustrates is a judicial duel between a man and a woman.

> The man stands in a circular pit up to his waist, armed with a club in his right hand, with which he assays to strike at the woman. He is severely prohibited, upon pain of forfeit, from stepping out of the pit. He may, however, steady himself with a hand on the edge of the pit or on the ground.
>
> The woman has a veil in her hand, in which a stone of several pounds is knotted. With them she attempts to strike at the man. As soon as the woman is able, she moves behind the man's back, endeavouring to drag his head to the edge of the pit and to strangle him. The woman strikes a blow with her veil, which the man parries with his club. But the veil wraps itself around the club and the woman seizes upon this advantage to wrench the club from the man's hand, disarming him, ending the combat and levying guilt unto the man.
>
> However, if the man parries the blow with his free left arm, he is presented with the opportunity to grab the woman about the waist, and to drag her into the pit, ending the fight unfavourably for her.[4]

In this particular duel, if the man is dragged from the pit or the woman into it, the 'forfeit' is to be taken off and immediately executed.

The majority of the manuscript deals with personal combat. Talhoffer includes lengthy illustrated passages on wrestling, unarmoured fighting with the long sword, messer (the 'long knife', a civilian weapon often pictured in Breugel's lively peasant scenes and similar to the hunting hanger, falchion, or ancient saxe), pole-axe, dagger, sword and buckler, and a series of mounted techniques. Talhoffer's manual amply proves that a unique, indigenous and systematic method of fencing and training with a wide array of weapons had developed in Germany during the Middle Ages, reaching its height in the fifteenth century. This is the German *Kunst des Fechten*, the 'art of fighting'.

THE GERMAN ART OF FIGHTING

Princes and Lords learn to survive with this art, in earnest and in play. But if you are fearful, then you should not learn to fence, because a despondent heart will always be defeated, regardless of all skill.[5]

Germany in the Middle Ages was a conglomeration of small principalities ruled by dynastic houses, bishoprics, municipal leagues, towns, and villages all struggling against each other for advantage and privilege. Warfare was a part of everyday life. Not only were there the full-scale wars of conquest and plunder sanctioned by the German Emperor, but petty 'private' wars also flourished at this time, fought between princeling and town, town and village, bishop and town, and every combination therein. Knights banded together into societies of self-interest and hired out their services. Renegade noblemen preyed upon travellers on the lonely trails through the dense German forests. Tradesmen and artisans in the larger towns formed fencing societies, which undertook the training and licensing of teachers. The two most famous of these societies, the *Marxbrüder* (The Brotherhood of St. Mark, of which the artist Albrecht Dürer was a member) and the *Federfechter*, provided champions to the court of the Holy Roman Emperor.[6] In Talhoffer's native Swabia, Count Eberhardt of Württemberg maintained one of the best military forces in Germany, consisting of a small knightly cavalry and an infantry levy of commoners trained on regular exercises and frequently lent to neighbouring powers.[7] The inherently violent nature of medieval society meant that no distinction was made between the civilian and military application of the German martial arts.

Medieval German swordsmanship pedagogy can be traced back directly to Johannes Liechtenauer, who lived during the fourteenth century.[8]

Liechtenauer travelled Europe to learn the mysteries of armed combat and devised a simple system of precepts for the long sword, which could be applied to every weapon. He put his teachings into verse and began the tradition of safeguarding the secrets of his art by obscuring his true meaning. After his death, his pupils began writing down his methods to prevent them from being corrupted, laying the groundwork for a strong and simple tradition of armed combat that would endure for almost three hundred years, until it was supplanted in the seventeenth century by the Italian 'thrust fencing' of the rapier that swept over Europe.

The German martial arts were divided into armoured, unarmoured and mounted fighting, all of which are represented by Talhoffer. His manuscript begins with a series of drawings on the use of the long sword before moving on to other weapons. Medieval swordplay was not the hacking, blade on blade, ring of steel affair represented in films and on the stage. Medieval swords were amazingly light and well balanced, weighing between only two to four pounds. Combatants in the Middle Ages used footwork, avoidance, and the ability to judge and manipulate timing and distance to exploit and enhance the sword's inherent cutting and thrusting capabilities. These skills were supplemented with techniques for grappling, wrestling, kicking and throwing the opponent, as well as disarming him by seizing his weapon. The primary tactical principle of the German art of fighting is to attack and defend in single time. In other words, every attack contains a defence and every defence contains a counter-attack.

An Overview of Medieval German Swordfighting

Holding the Sword
The sword is held with the right hand close to the cross guard. The left hand rests below the right, and controls the levering actions of the sword. The left hand may also cup the fig-shaped pommel for more manoeuvrability and reach, and to increase the power of thrusts. The sword is held for the most part with the edges up and down, perpendicular to the ground.

Stance
The swordsman faces his opponent squarely, with his hips and torso parallel to him, and his legs slightly bent. He may stand with either leg slightly forward.

Footwork
The footwork is as simple and direct as walking. The fighter steps naturally

forward and back, from side to side and diagonally, and pivots on one leg or another to circle his opponent. Footwork is used to maintain distance, avoid blows, and close in for attacks. All cuts are accompanied by a step, either forward or back.

Cuts

Cuts are divided into cuts from above and cuts from below (*oberhau* and *underhau*), as in plate 1. Cuts are made most often with the 'true' edge, the lower edge aligned with the knuckles, but may also be made with the 'false' edge, the upper edge aligned with the thumbs. There are three kinds of cuts: powerful cuts from the shoulders and body, medium cuts from the elbows, and harassing cuts made from the wrists and hands. Footwork is directly tied to cutting, which Talhoffer addresses in plate 9 with the caption, 'This is the strong way to fight going left to right.' This is a reference to the fact that the combatant must step into each cut, so that the weight of the body and torque of the hips may help deliver it successfully. With a cut from the left to the right, the swordsman must step forward with the left foot as the cut lands.[9]

Thrusts

It is surprising how many thrusts Talhoffer shows, as the medieval sword is thought of as primarily a cutting weapon. However, it is evident from this manuscript that the German art of fighting placed a heavy emphasis on actions along the opposing blade resulting in thrusts. As with the cuts, thrusts come from above and below. Thrusts are most often aimed at the two lower 'openings' or targets in the soft parts below the ribcage, on the right and left side of the body (plates 6 and 14). They may also be aimed at the two upper openings, on the right and left of the body above the line of the ribcage. Other targets include the wrists, the feet, the thighs and the face.

Guards

Talhoffer illustrates a number of guards, wards or stances, each with a characteristically colourful mnemonic name. Thus, we have the 'iron gate' (plate 16), the 'squinting' guard (plate 36), and the 'fire-poker' (plate 39). The guards are not static positions of defence. Rather, they are moments of transition from which cuts and thrusts begin or end. The guards are fluid, flowing from one to another, and should be thought of as positions from which to initiate attacks.

The four basic guards in the German art of fighting are the low or 'iron gate' guard; the middle guard or the 'plough', with the sword hilt held in front of the body at waist height with the point directed toward the enemy; the right and left hanging guards or 'oxen', with the sword hilt held at the side of the head and the blade lowered diagonally across the body and

directed toward the enemy (plate 13); and the high guard, with the sword
held directly above the head, pointing back at a 45-degree angle and from
which cuts may be made *von tach*, or 'from the roof'.

Attack and Counter-Attack

As mentioned above, the primary tactical principle of the German art of
fighting is that for every attack there is a counter-attack (*stuck und bruch*).
Attacks are met with counter-cuts and thrusts that set aside the enemy's
weapon to force a way through the enemy's guard. Counter-attacks may be
combined with avoidance, grappling, wrestling and disarms to render the
opponent defenceless.

Avoidance

The first means of defence open to the swordsman is to avoid the attack: to
be where the sword is not. This may be accomplished by stepping back out
of distance. However, a cutting sword moves with the most force at the point
of percussion, a few inches below the point, and with the least force near the
hands. Therefore, a more effective technique for avoidance is to close the
distance by stepping toward the opponent, moving straight in or diagonally
to either side, and counter-attacking, grappling, or making a disarm.

Setting Aside

Attacks may be countered by setting them aside with the blade, or
versetzen. Similar to the modern fencing 'parry', setting aside is an action
that deflects the oncoming steel by either cutting directly into it to strike
the opponent, or by redirecting its force with the blade to gain an
advantage over him. Talhoffer never shows anything resembling static,
blade on blade blocks. His setting aside techniques are fluid and dynamic,
and lead naturally into counter-attacks.

Grappling

Nearly a third of Talhoffer's long sword plates include some form of
grappling. When the distance between the combatants is closed suddenly,
the sword becomes ineffective. Grappling is used to regain proper fighting
distance, to throw the opponent off balance, and to disarm him.

Binds and Weak vs Strong

Talhoffer illustrates many techniques that come from a bind or crossing of
the swords with opposition (plates 29–32, among others). Once the swords
are bound or crossed, a deadly game of leverage begins. The sword is
naturally 'weak' near the point and 'strong' near the hands, so a swordsman
may lever his opponent's blade by applying the strong part of his sword to
the weak part of his enemy's sword. There are also weak and strong forces

of opposition. In a bind, the swordsman may apply a weak force to his opponent's strong force and allow the enemy steel to pass through the bind, freeing his own blade for attack. In addition, strong pressure may be applied in order to break through the opponent's guard or to use the enemy's sword as a guide to direct thrusts at the opponent's body.

Half-Sword
The half-sword techniques were originally devised for fighting armoured opponents (plate 26). The sword is gripped on the blade with the left hand and used like a short spear or bayonet to slice or stab into the armpits, groin, face, throat and joints. The superior leverage of the half-sword may also be used to perform actions on the opponent's blade, setting it aside or trapping it.

In emergencies, the sword may be reversed to thrust the pommel at the opponent's face (plate 38), or held by the blade with both hands to use the cross hilt to hook, trip or disarm. The reversed sword may also be wielded like a large hammer, resulting in terrifying blows called the 'murder stroke' or *mortschlag*, and 'thunderclap stroke' or *donnerschlag* (plates 33 and 37).

The techniques described above for the long sword may be applied to any hand-held weapon. You will note half-sword actions used with the pole-axe, setting aside techniques with the duelling shields, grappling with the messer. Every weapon in Talhoffer's arsenal is wielded in the four basic guards and used to make cuts and thrusts from below and above.

The German art of fighting is simple, direct and effective. It has only one object: the swift demise of the enemy by any means.

TALHOFFER'S ARSENAL

Long Sword
(plates 1–67, 74–8)
The long sword, war sword, hand-and-a-half sword, or bastard sword is the chief weapon of Talhoffer's arsenal, and the fundamental techniques for its use may be applied to every other weapon in his book. The long sword is between four and four-and-a-half feet in length with a sharply tapered double-edged blade of diamond profile, a simple cross hilt, a fig-shaped pommel, and a handle long enough to be gripped with one or both hands. This weapon is surprisingly light, capable of making blindingly fast attacks, and is suitable for both cuts and thrusts. As the

plates illustrate, the entire sword is used, either by gripping the blade with the off-hand for strong half-sword attacks, or reversing it to strike with the pommel or to employ the hilt as a hammer to batter through the opponent's defences.

Armoured Fight with Spear and Long Sword
(plates 68–73)
The armoured fight with spear and sword is a judicial combat between noblemen in full plate armour. They begin the ritual by sitting on a platform in the lists (the barriers surrounding the duelling ground) and displaying their weapons, with their attendants beside them and their coffins before them. The spear is used as the primary weapon, with the sword held in reserve for the *coup de grâce*.

Pole-Axe
(plates 79–103)
The pole-axe is most commonly used in armoured fighting, and is specifically designed as an 'armour-breaker'. Talhoffer, however, shows it in unarmoured fight. Talhoffer's weapon is a 'Lucerne Hammer': a long staff weapon with a notched hammer head surmounted and surrounded by sharp spikes. The shaft is used to trip the opponent by sweeping his legs, or to thrust him in the head or chest. The spikes at the side and back are used to hook and drag the opponent to the ground, and the long, blade-like spike on top is used to make killing thrusts. Although the pole-axe is primarily a knightly weapon, the techniques for its use are equally applicable to the axe-bladed halberd, the weapon of choice for the select combatants held in reserve for counter-attack in the centre of the formidable pike formations of the Swiss Confederates and German *Landsknechte*.[10]

Duelling Shield
(plates 104–64)
The duelling shield is used in judicial combat. It is a slightly concave oblong, approximately six-and-a-half feet tall, with a rectangular coffered boss along the longitudinal axis allowing room for the hand to grip a central pole, which is sharply spiked at both ends. The shield is made of wood, possibly covered with cloth or leather, and bears the image of the cross. It is used both defensively and offensively to deflect blows and hammer into the opponent's shield to create openings, as well as to stab with the spikes. The combatants are barefoot and sewn into tight-fitting cowled leather suits with a red cross on their chests and backs and the back of their cowls. When fighting according to the Frankish law, the combatants use a large wooden mace with their shields. When fighting according to the Swabian law, they employ the long sword.

Throated Hooking Shield
(plates 165–9)
The throated hooking shield is perhaps the most unusual weapon in Talhoffer's arsenal. It is a cello-shaped affair with four protruding hooks at the top and bottom for catching, pulling and stabbing the adversary. Like the simple duelling shield, it has a sharply-spiked central pole which may be used to impale the opponent.

Dagger
(plates 170–89)
The dagger is the ultimate weapon of last resort. Talhoffer shows the rondel variety with an extremely long, triangular blade and a grip with two flanges at top and bottom to protect the hand. The dagger is the simplest and most commonly carried weapon of medieval Germany. Techniques are illustrated for using the dagger to shield against stabs, gripping the blade with the off-hand to create locks on the opponent's dagger, blocking with both the dagger arm and the off-hand, and grappling.

Wrestling
(plates 190–221)
Nearly a third of the armed combat plates show some kind of wrestling or grappling, and Talhoffer devotes thirty-two plates to wrestling alone. Wrestling is essential to the German art of fighting, since the fight must become hand-to-hand once distance is closed within the effective range of the weapons, or if either of the combatants should be disarmed. Talhoffer borrows his wrestling techniques from Ott, an earlier wrestling master to the Habsburg Dukes of Austria.[11]

Messer
(plates 223–30)
The messer, or 'long knife', has a short, single-edged blade with a simple cross hilt. The blade is slightly curved and the last few inches of the clipped back or false edge are sharp. It is carried in one hand, with the other hand held behind the back as in modern sabre fencing. The messer resembles the ancient saxe, falchion, the Italian storta, the Bohemian dusak (a wooden training weapon used in Germany into the seventeenth century), the Polish sabre, and the modern machete. Commoners in medieval Germany carried it as an everyday side-arm. The messer is capable of making shearing cuts fierce enough to remove a hand from the arm, as can be seen in plate 228. Albrecht Dürer devotes a large section of his *Fechtbuch* to the messer (see bibliography).

Sword and Buckler
(plates 231–41)
We get the word 'swashbuckler' from the British proclivity for the sword
and buckler. This weapon combination was in use across Europe since the
twelfth century. The oldest fencing manual in existence, the anonymous
thirteenth-century German manuscript I.33 in the collection of the British
Museum, is entirely devoted to the sword and buckler. The buckler is a
small, round shield with a central boss (a bowl-shaped protrusion allowing
room for the hand) and handle. It is used with a single-handed sword with
a simple cross hilt and a large circular pommel. Talhoffer's buckler is rather
ornate, with two hook-like protrusions at the top and bottom for catching
and deflecting the oncoming blade. At the end of this section, Talhoffer
shows techniques for one man fighting against two.

Combat between a Man and a Woman
(plates 242–50)
The fight between a man and a woman, as described above (pp.10–11), is
another judicial duel in which the man is placed up to his waist in a pit and
armed with a large wooden mace. The woman is free to move around him
on the ground, and is armed with a three- or four-pound stone knotted
into a long veil.

Mounted Combat
(plates 251–70)
The final series of plates shows methods of mounted combat with the long
sword, long sword against the lance, lance against crossbow, and mounted
hand-to-hand fighting.

FOR THE MODERN READER

The Western martial heritage, encompassing a broad array of weapons,
each with its own sophisticated methodology, is being rediscovered by a
new generation of fencers. Scholars, students and practitioners all over the
world are devoting time and study to reviving European armed combat as
a living martial art. Forgotten and neglected ancient fencing manuals are
being dusted off and used by modern swordsmen and women to apply
historically accurate techniques to train and fence with edged and pole
weapons long dismissed from the arsenal of the conventional fencer.

Talhoffer's book provides us with an unparalleled visual reference.
Each drawing is a carefully composed snapshot isolated in time, revealing
the elegant intricacies of the German art of fighting. The illustrations may

be thought of as flash-cards to prompt the memory, and may be rearranged to discover connections and sequences of action. Used in conjunction with other manuals of this period which are richer in text, such as those by Sigmund Ringeck (*c*1440), Fiore dei Liberi (*c*1410) and Joachim Meyer (1570), we are able to reconstruct these personal combat techniques as they were actually practised in the Middle Ages. This book was meant to be used. And it can be used by the modern martial artist, but only by working through it carefully, with full respect for the martial heritage it represents and the dangerous and lethal nature of the skills it would impart.

For the stage and film fight combatant or choreographer, this *Fechtbuch* offers an exciting vocabulary of moves, actions and weapons, many of which have never before been seen by an audience. Because Talhoffer's techniques are authentic, they are bio-mechanically sound and easy to learn and practise safely. They can be exploited to enliven the tired 'parry and riposte', edge-gouging swordplay so common in the theatre and on the screen today.

Beyond this manuscript's appeal for the martial artist or stage swordsman, it possesses great aesthetic beauty and historical interest. We do not know for certain who drew the figures in Talhoffer's manuals. Whether it was Talhoffer himself or some anonymous Swabian scribe, the artist took painstaking care to give each of the figures life and expression. We are treated to images of everyday dress, with doublet, codpiece, hose, a variety of headgear and the extravagantly pointed shoes of the late Middle Ages; full suits of armour; ritual battle dress; and equestrian equipage. This book is a time machine, providing us with a glimpse of real people really fighting with all the skill, sophistication and ruthlessness of the *Kunst des Fechten*.

To paraphrase Gustav Hergsell, if I succeed in bringing the art lover, historian, fencer and stage combatant closer together through this priceless artifact of the German Middle Ages, I will have achieved my goal.

Mark Rector
2000

Notes

1. Swabia was an ancient province lying between the upper reaches of the Danube and the Rhine, whose territories included Baden-Württemberg, the Black Forest, and parts of Western Bavaria and northern Switzerland. It was the seat of the powerful Staufen and Hohenzollern families.

2. Gustav Hergsell, *Talhoffers Fechtbuch aus dem Jahre 1467*, Prague, 1887. Translations from Hergsell throughout this book are by Mark Rector.

3. The last claim to a 'wager of battel' in Great Britain was made in 1818 by an accused murderer. His challenge went unaccepted and he escaped the gibbet. The next year, Parliament repealed the law permitting judicial duels. (From Andrew Steinmetz, *The Romance of Duelling*, 1868.)

4. Gustav Hergsell, *Talhoffers Fechtbuch aus dem Jahre 1467*, Prague, 1887.

5. Master Sigmund Ringeck, *Fechtbuch* (*c*1440). Translation by Jörg Bellinghausen.

6. Gustav Hergsell, *Talhoffers Fechtbuch aus dem Jahre 1467*, Prague, 1887.

7. F.R.H. Du Boulay, *Germany in the Later Middle Ages*, 1983.

8. S. Matthew Galas, 'Kindred Spirits', *Journal of Asian Martial Arts*, Vol. 6 No. 3, 1997.

9. Talhoffer illustrates combatants employing a right-hand lead throughout his book. If the left-handed fencer is uncomfortable managing the sword in this manner, he or she should simply perform the techniques as a mirror image of the drawings, holding the sword with the left hand nearest the cross guard and using the right hand for grips and grappling. The fundamental elements of the German art of fighting remain the same.

10. C.W.C. Oman, *A History of the Art of War in the Middle Ages*, 1924, 1991.

11. S. Matthew Galas, 'Kindred Spirits', *Journal of Asian Martial Arts*, Vol. 6 No. 3, 1997.

MEDIEVAL COMBAT

I. LONG SWORD:[1] PLATES 1–67

The swordsman on the left cuts from above. The swordsman on the right cuts from below.

Plate 1

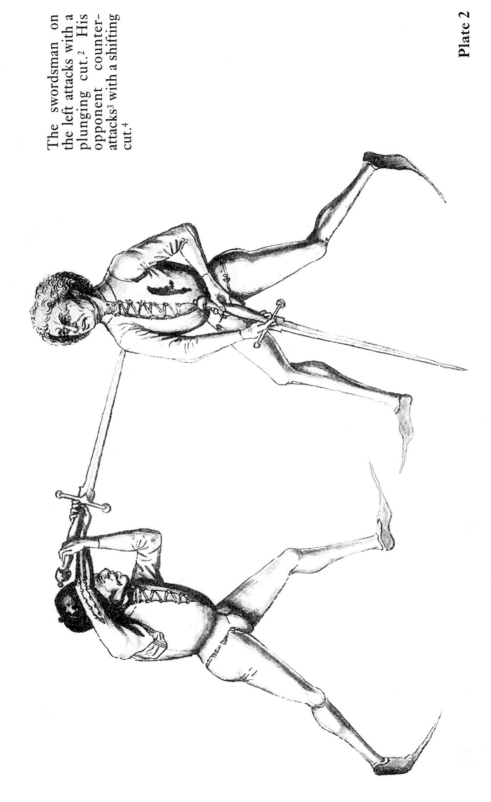

The swordsman on the left attacks with a plunging cut.[2] His opponent counter-attacks[3] with a shifting cut.[4]

Plate 2

The swordsman on the left menaces his opponent with the thrust of wrath.[5] The swordsman on the right counters the thrust with a cut from above.

Plate 3

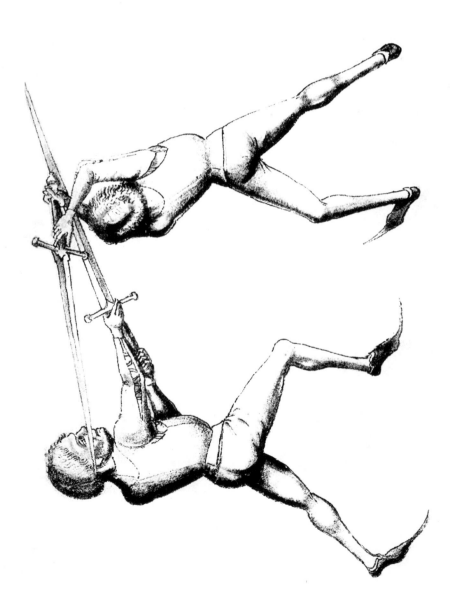

The swordsman on the left throws a long thrust of wrath. His opponent counters by making a crosswise thrust.[6]

Plate 4

The swordsman on the left makes an open or exposed cut from above (*von tach* or from the roof).[7] His opponent counters the attack with a slash to the throat.

Plate 5

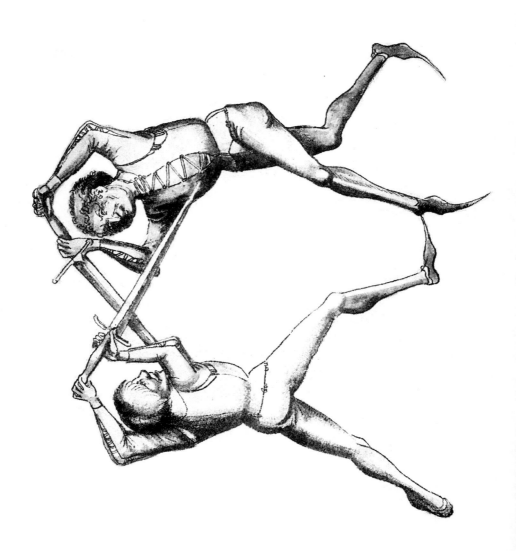

Downward thrusts to the lower openings or targets.[8]

Plate 6

The swordsman on the left captures his opponent's sword.

Plate 7

'A placement, or to get there first.' The swordsman on the right counters his opponent's cut by placing his blade on target before the on-coming blow arrives.

Plate 8

This is the strong way to fight going left to right.[9]

Plate 9

The swordsman on the left makes an open or exposed thrust. The swordsman on the right springs his sword at his opponent, throwing it suddenly outward while maintaining hold of the pommel with his left hand.

Plate 10

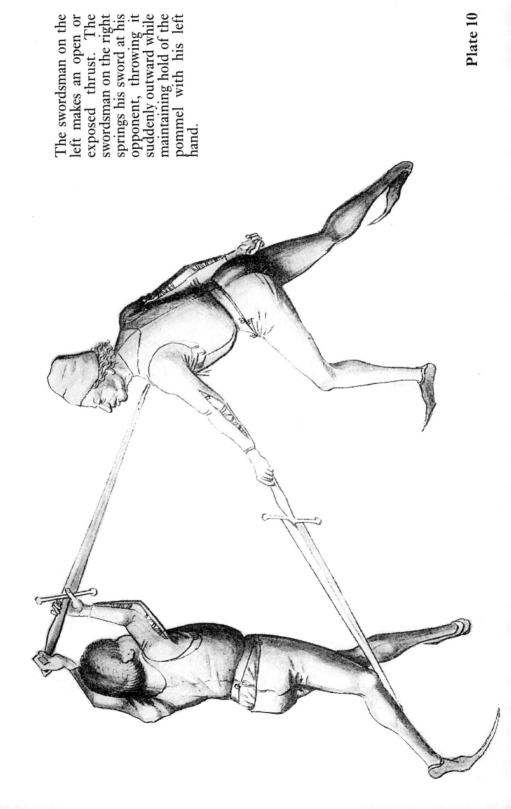

From a bind or crossing of the swords, the swordsman on the left shoves his opponent away by grasping him behind the elbow (see plate 32).[10]

Plate 11

The swordsman on the right closes in upon his opponent with an open or exposed thrust and kicks him in the belly.

Plate 12

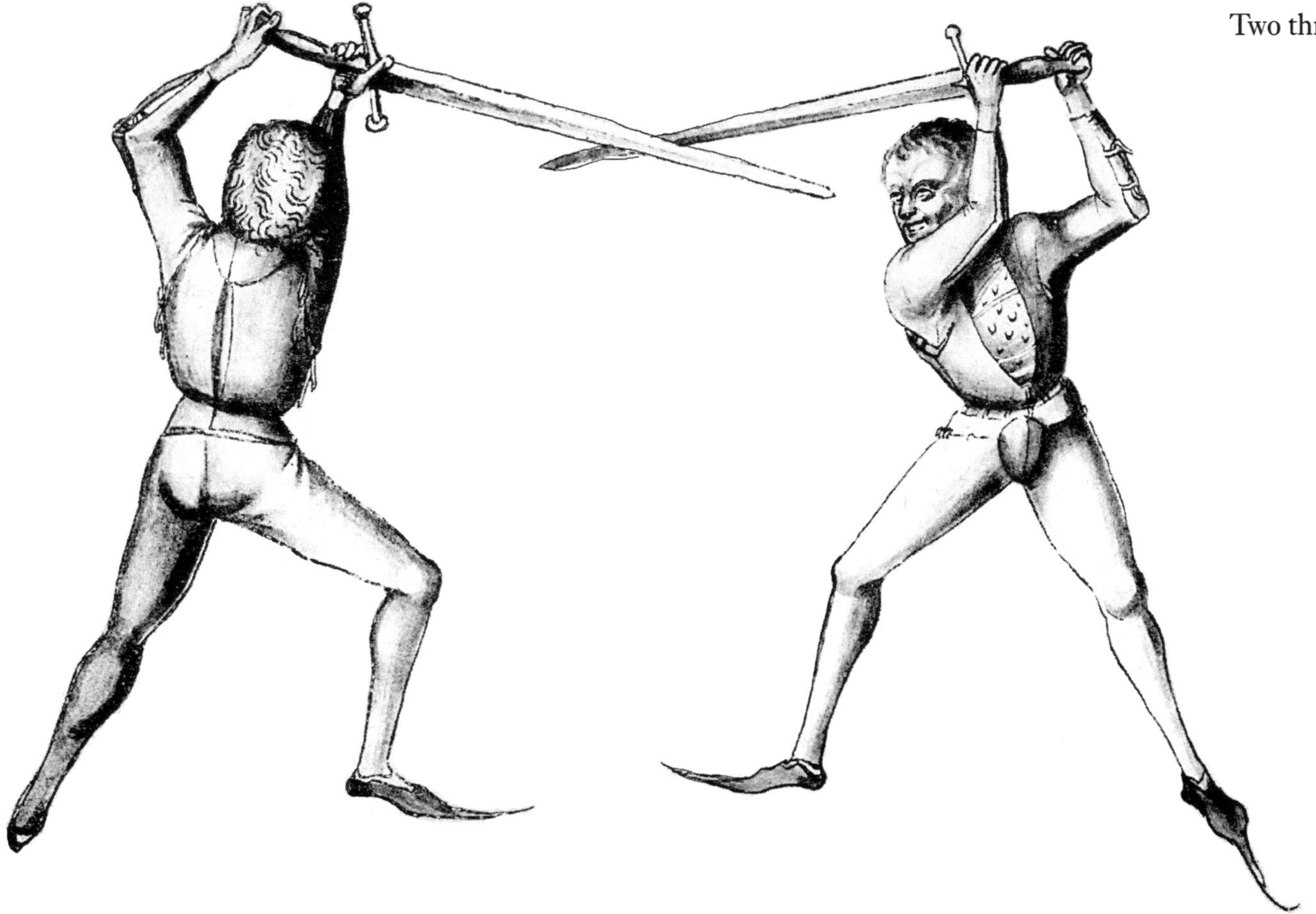

Two thrusts from above.

Plate 13

The two lower openings
or targets (see note 8).

Plate 14

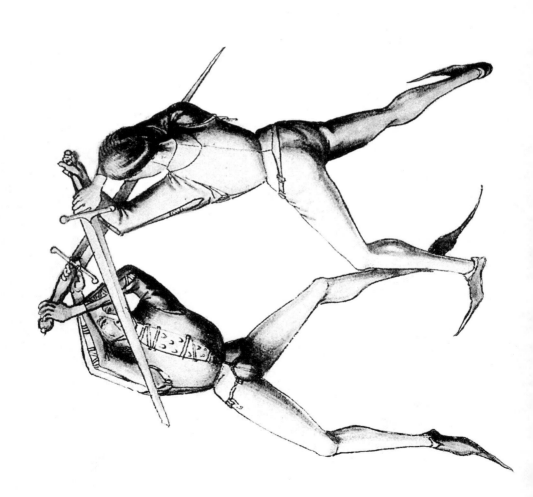

The swordsman on the right counters his opponent's attack by dashing his opponent's sword away from right to left, releasing his own right hand from his sword. From here, he will step in to grapple his adversary.

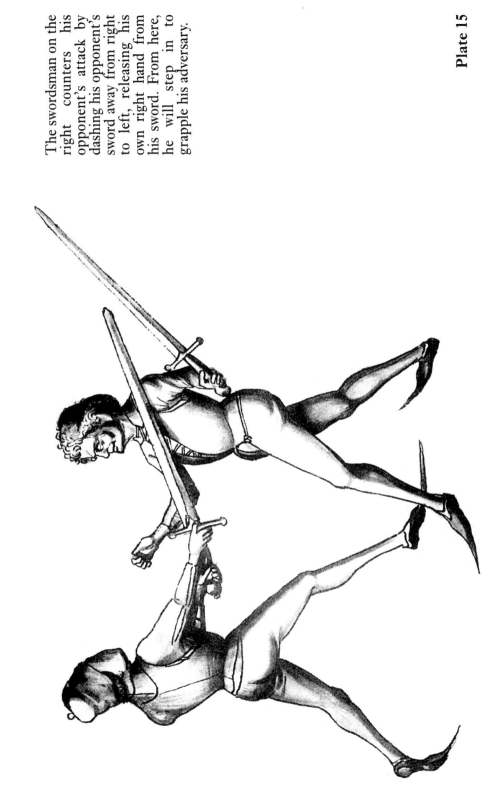

Plate 15

The swordsman on the right stands in the iron gate guard.[11] His opponent attacks above the iron gate guard.

Plate 16

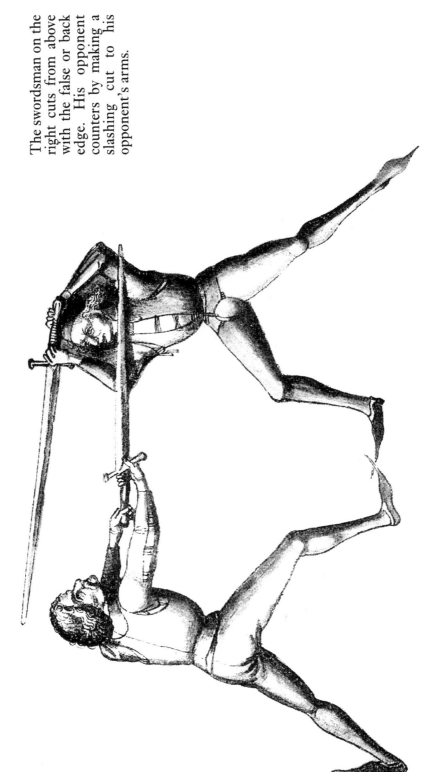

The swordsman on the right cuts from above with the false or back edge. His opponent counters by making a slashing cut to his opponent's arms.

Plate 17

The swordsman on the left makes a crosswise thrust (see note 6). His opponent cuts from above.

Plate 18

The nimble crooked cut.[12] Counter-attack by turning the point against it.

Plate 19

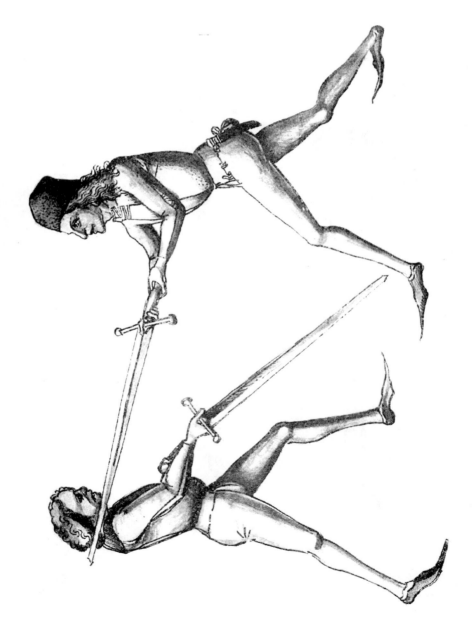

The swordsman on the right completes the crooked cut.

Plate 20

The swordsman on the left attacks toward his opponent's lower opening. The swordsman on the right counters by slicing into the attack from above.

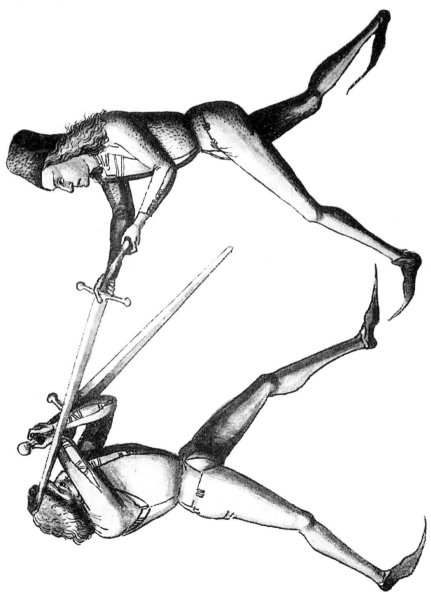

Plate 21

Plate 22

War Work[13]

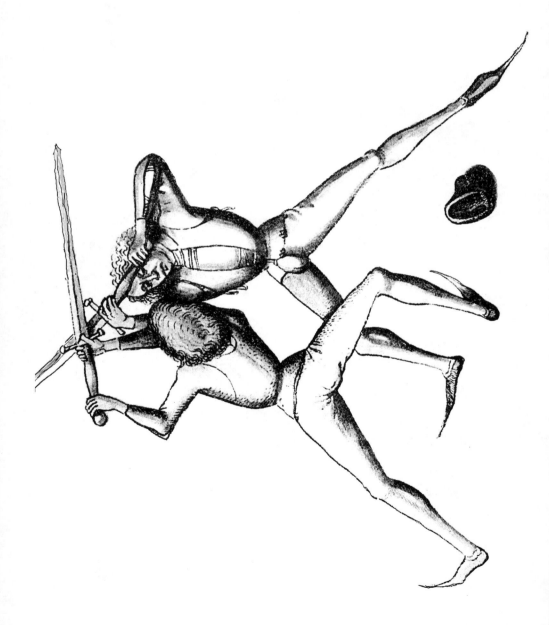

The swordsman on the left is in a weak crosswise guard. His opponent stands in a strong right hanging guard.[14]

Plate 23

A sudden attack. The swordsman on the right quickly closes in upon his opponent.

Plate 24

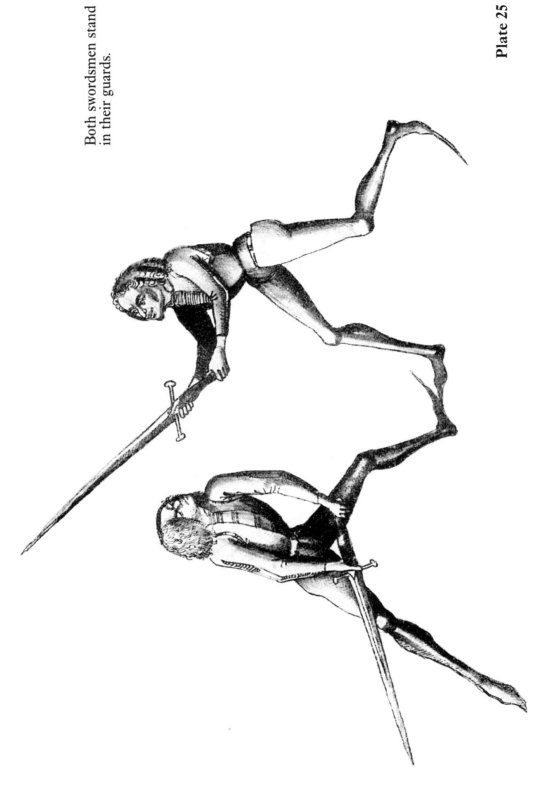

Both swordsmen stand
in their guards.

Plate 25

The swordsman on the left steps forward at the half-sword and traps his opponent's blade.[15]

Plate 26

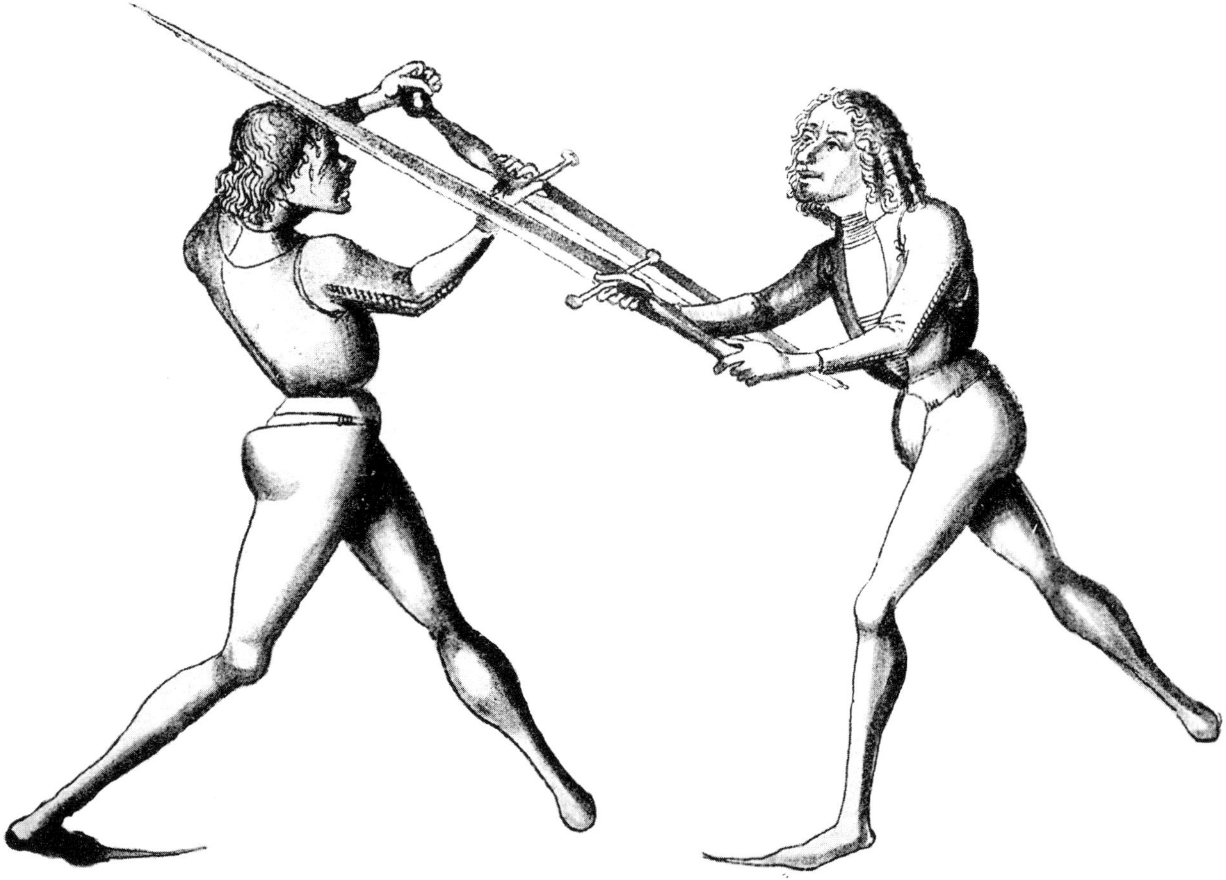

The swordsman on the left stands with his point free to thrust. His opponent counters by cutting over the point to the left.

Plate 27

The swordsman on the left steps quickly into a half-sword thrust to counter his opponent's cut from above.

Plate 28

Against a bind rush in, grapple and throw your opponent.

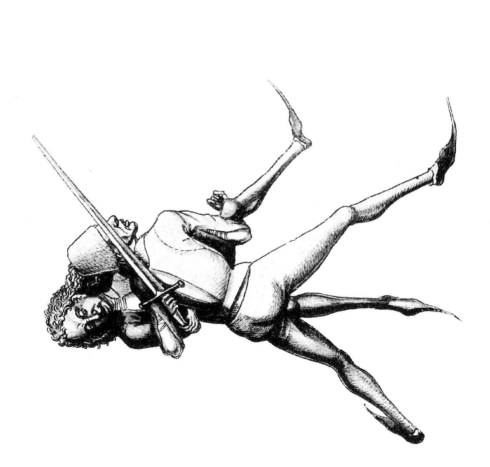

Plate 29

Another forceful grapple against the bind.[16]

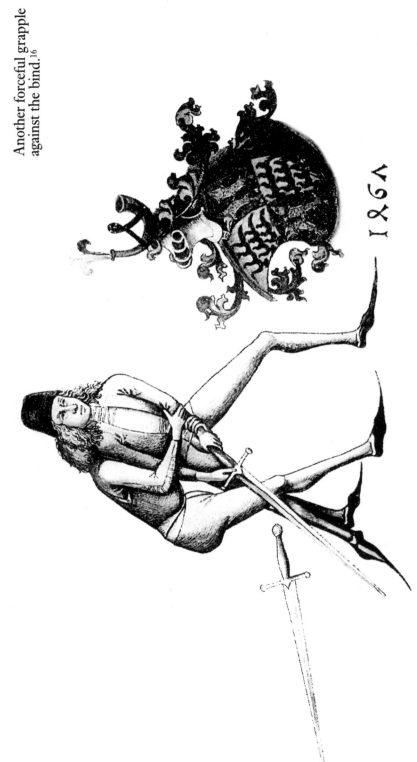

Plate 30

From a bind, the swordsman on the right steps quickly forward with a downward thrust.

Plate 31

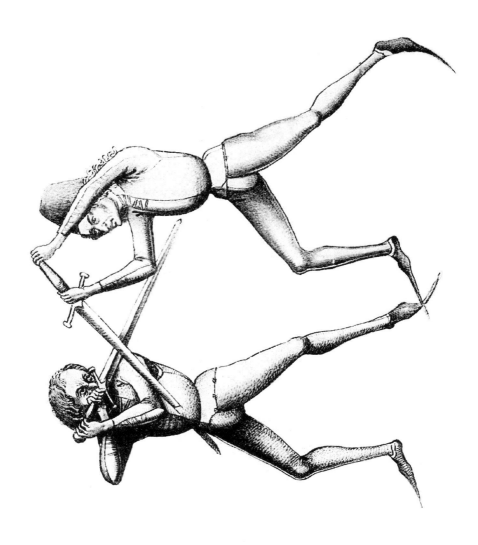

From a bind, the swords-
man on the left shoves
his opponent away by
grasping him behind the
elbow (see plate 11).

Plate 32

The murder-stroke.[17]

Plate 33

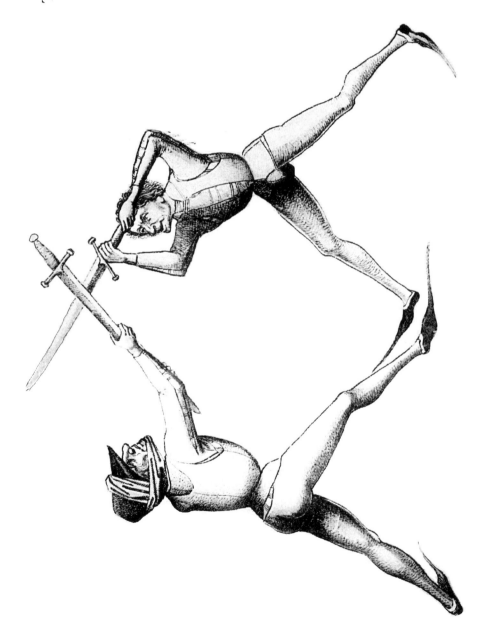

A wrestling throw following a murder-stroke.

Plate 34

The swordsman on the left steps quickly forward into a half-sword thrust to counter his opponent's cut from above.

Plate 35

The swordsman on the left steps quickly forward into a half-sword thrust from the squinting guard.[18]

Plate 36

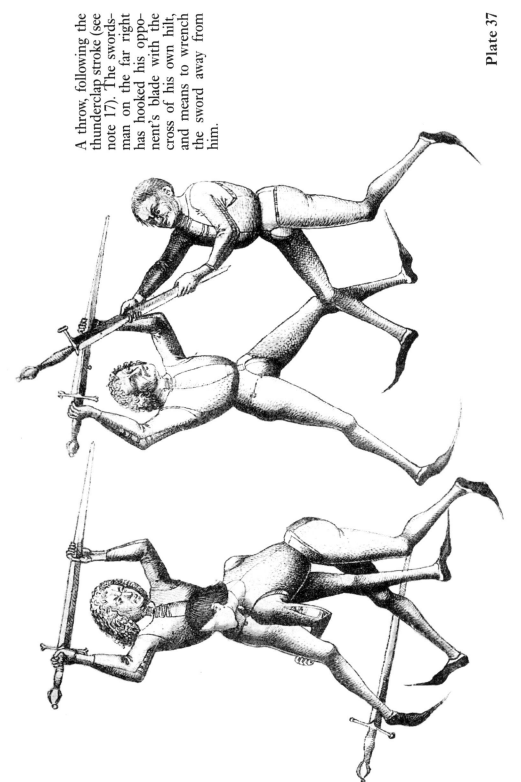

A throw, following the thunderclap stroke (see note 17). The swordsman on the far right has hooked his opponent's blade with the cross of his own hilt, and means to wrench the sword away from him.

Plate 37

The swordsman on the left thrusts at his opponent's face with the pommel of his sword, having wrenched his opponent's blade away from him.

Plate 38

The *brentschirn*, or the bind with the shortened sword.[19]

Plate 39

An action countering the bind with the shortened sword. (It appears that the swordsman on the left is about to cut his opponent's blade away from him.)

Plate 40

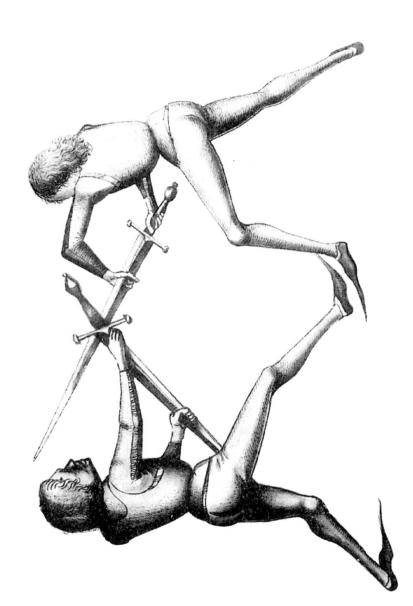

The swordsman on the right leans in with his left elbow from the *brentschüren*, or bind with the shortened sword, to counter his opponent's reversed-sword attack.

Plate 41

Aggressive half-sword stances for thrusting from above and below.

Plate 42

Crowding in to the work, or in-fighting, with the half-sword.

Plate 43

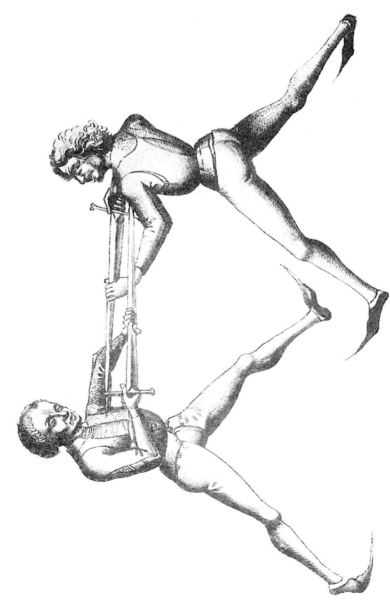

The swordsman on the right stabs his opponent's wrist.

Plate 44

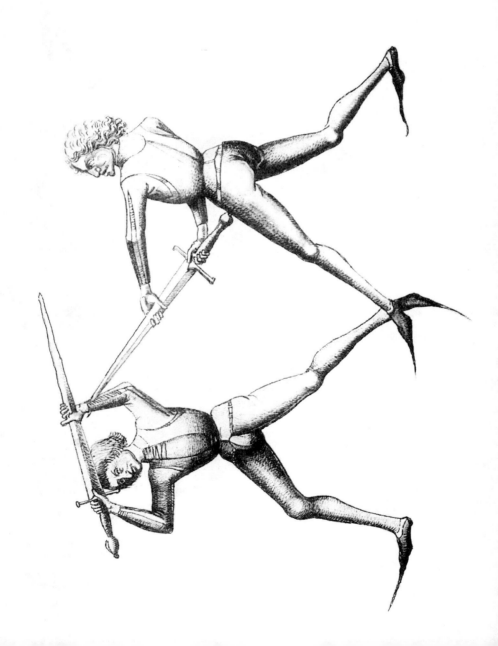

The swordsman on the left stabs his opponent's foot.

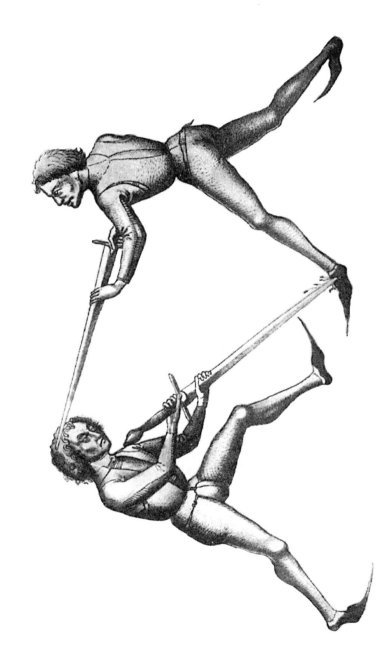

Plate 45

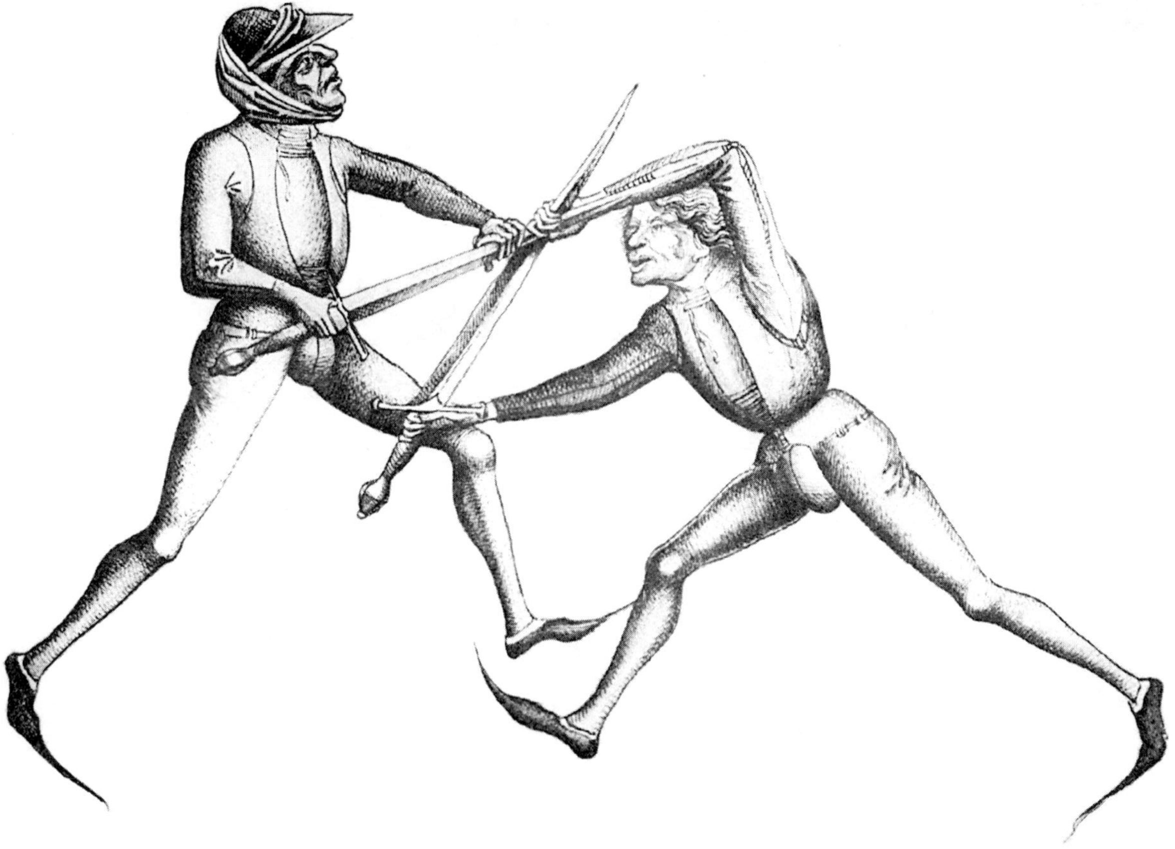

The swordsman on the right moves out of the bind to wrench the hollow of his opponent's knee with the hilt of his sword.

Plate 46

The swordsman on the right makes a false murder-stroke, and cuts his opponent on the thigh.[20]

Plate 47

The swordsman on the right moves out of the bind to wrench the hilt of his sword into his opponent's throat.

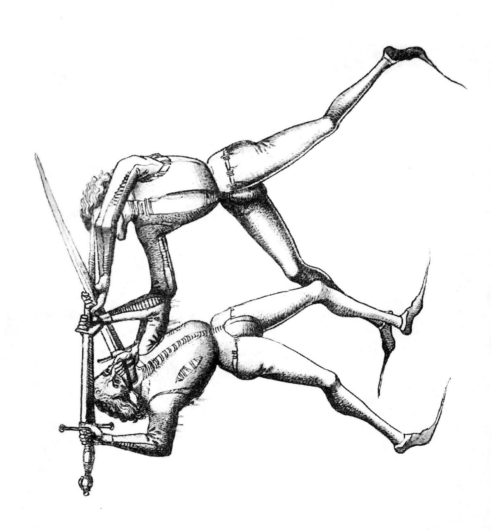

Plate 48

The swordsmen have seized each other's blades.[21]

Plate 49

The combatant on the left captures his opponent's sword.

Plate 50

Shifting the sword.[22]

Plate 51

The swordsman on the right thrusts with his pommel to catch his opponent's blade with his hilt and wrench it away from him.

Plate 52

The swordsman on the left sets aside his opponent's murder-stroke and wrenches his pommel into his opponent's throat.[23]

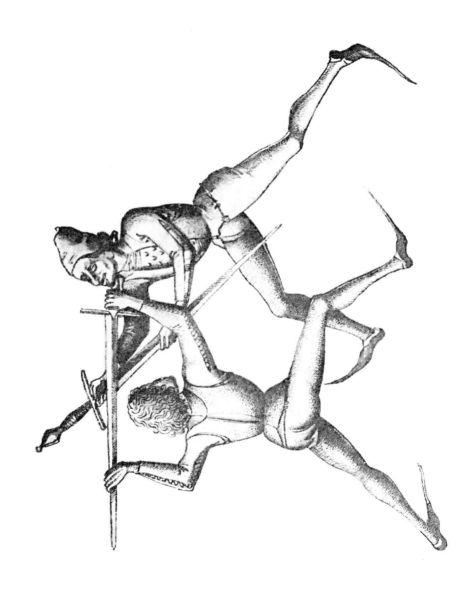

Plate 53

The swordsman on the left makes an entanglement from the *brentschiren* or the bind with the short-ened sword, resulting in a thrust to his opponent's chest.

Plate 54

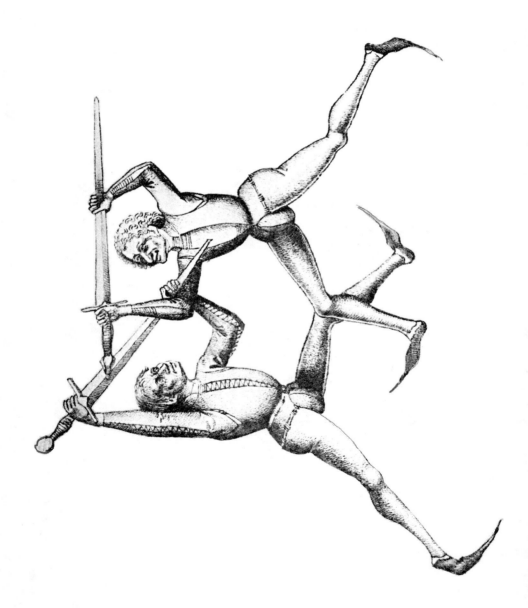

Having had his sword seized, the swordsman on the right throws both his sword and opponent away from himself and means to finish him off by grappling him.

Plate 55

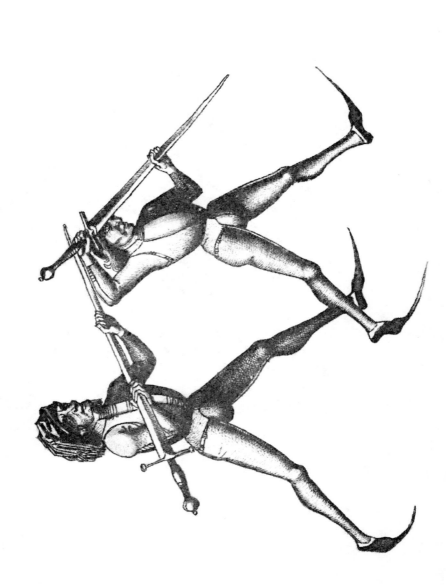

The combatant on the right avoids his opponent's murder-stroke by turning away.

Plate 56

Having avoided the murder-stroke, the combatant on the right counters by grappling and throwing his opponent.

Plate 57

After making the murder-stroke, the swordsman on the right avoids his opponent's thrust and hooks him behind the neck with the cross of his sword to wrench him to the ground.

Plate 58

Having seized his opponent's blade, the swordsman on the left slides his own blade along it (bracing himself with his right foot on the small of his opponent's back).

Plate 59

From the *brentschürn* or the bind with the shortened sword, the swordsman on the right locks his opponent's blade and prepares to throw him.

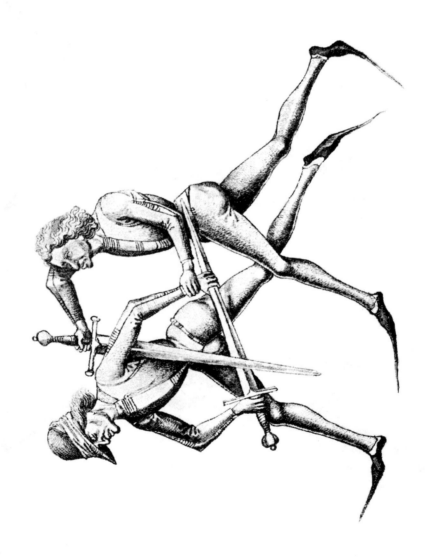

Plate 60

The high and low-reversed half-sword stances for making and warding stabs and cuts.

Plate 61

Another sword capture.

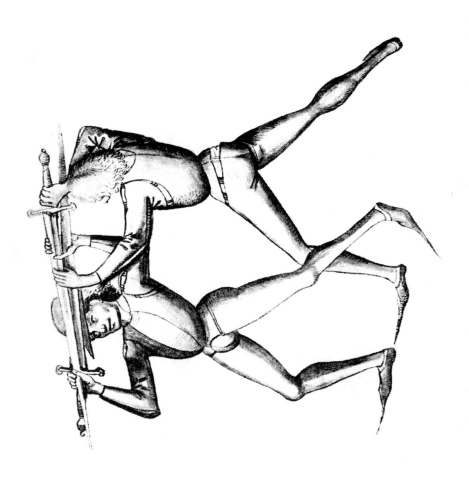

Plate 62

The swordsman on the left intends to strike. The swordsman on the right prepares to charge in upon his opponent.

Plate 63

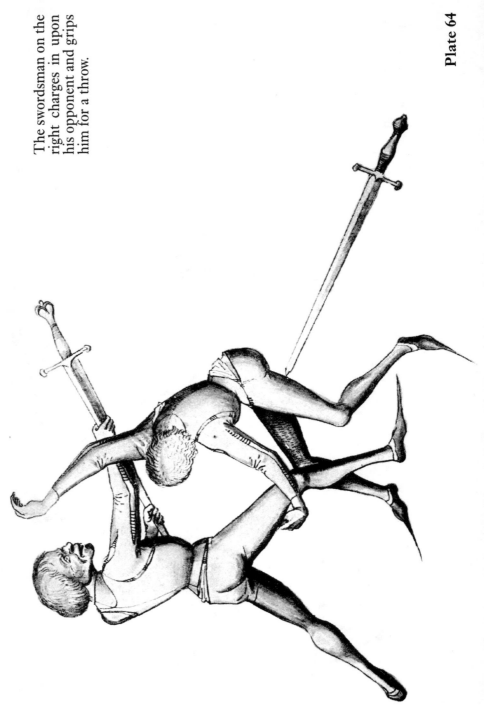

The swordsman on the right charges in upon his opponent and grips him for a throw.

Plate 64

The throw is achieved.

Plate 65

The swordsman on the right sets aside his opponent's thrust and wrenches his sword hilt into his opponent's arm.

Plate 66

The swordsman on the right steps forward at the half-sword toward his opponent and thrusts him in the face with the pommel of his sword.

Plate 67

II. ARMOURED COMBAT IN THE LISTS WITH SPEAR AND SWORD:[24] PLATES 68–73

An armoured combatant enters the lists. His attendant displays his banner and equipment.

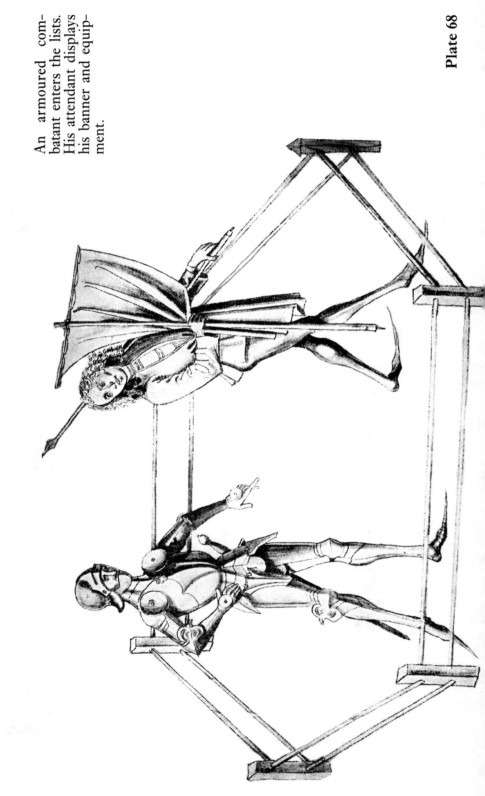

Plate 68

Both combatants sit in the lists awaiting the commencement of the trial by combat. Each has his attendant beside him and his coffin before him.[25]

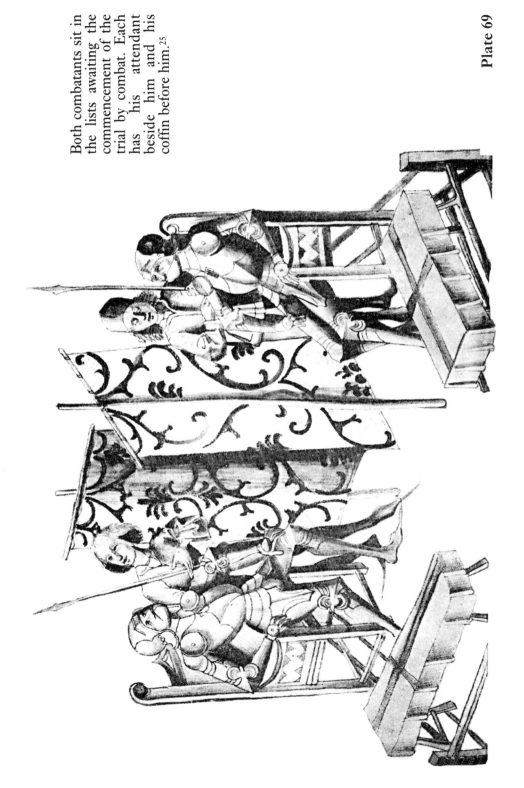

Plate 69

As the trial begins, the combatant on the right prepares to throw his spear. The combatant on the left stands on guard to receive his opponent's attack.

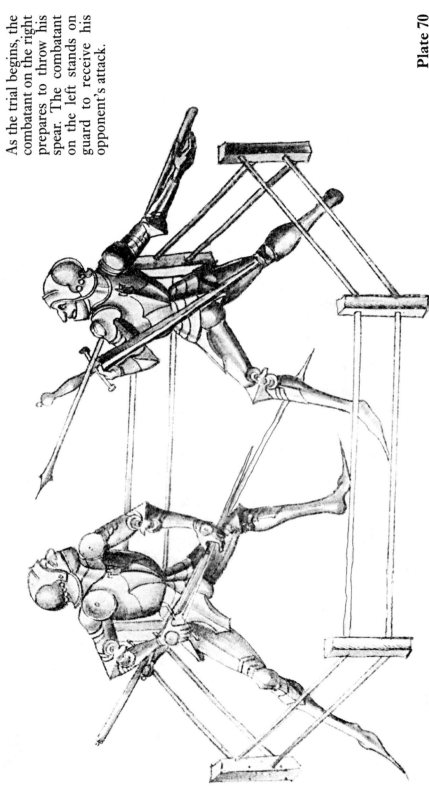

Plate 70

The combatant on the left throws his spear. The combatant on the right sets it aside, using his sword and spear together.

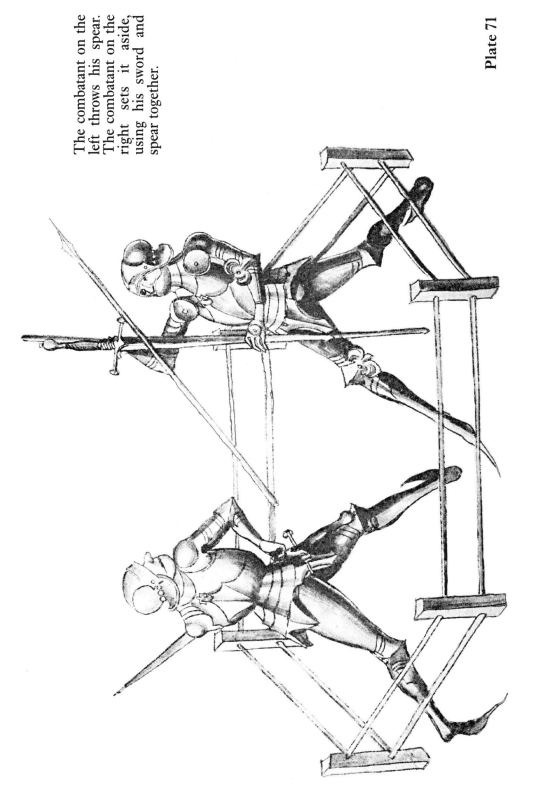

Plate 71

The combatant on the right charges in with a murder-stroke. The combatant on the left prepares to set aside the blow.

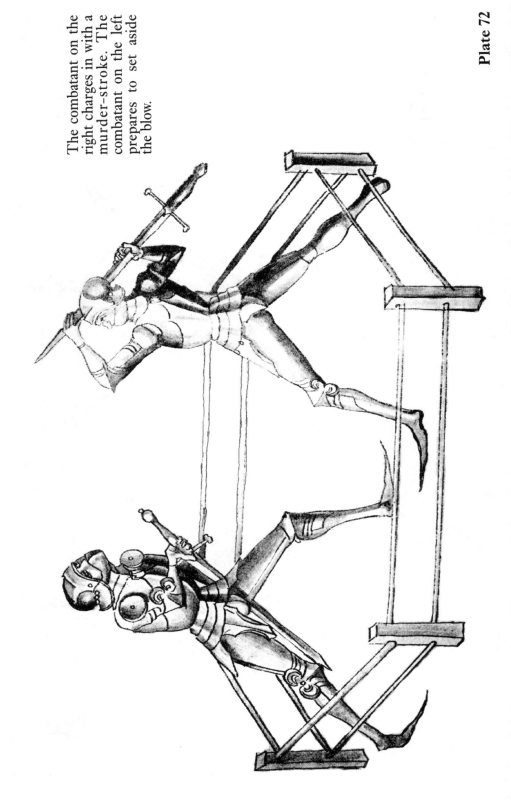

Plate 72

The murder-stroke lands on the defender's sword. The combatant on the left will now thrust to his opponent's face.

Plate 73

III. LONG SWORD: PLATES 74–78

The swordsman on the right steps forward to throw his opponent over his thigh.

Plate 74

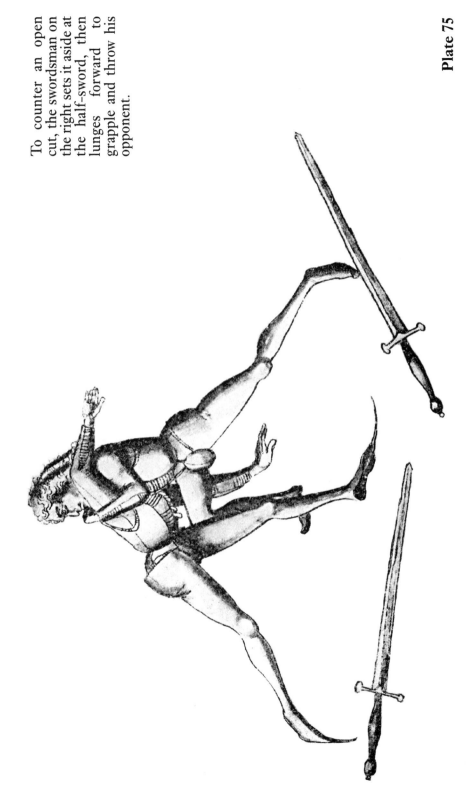

To counter an open cut, the swordsman on the right sets it aside at the half-sword, then lunges forward to grapple and throw his opponent.

Plate 75

Attack and counter-
attack.[26]

Plate 76

From left to right: A desperate stabbing attack. – The proper stance to receive such an attack. – This swordsman is ready to fight. – This is an advantageous stance for a disarmed man.

Plate 77

The pair on the left wrestle for control of the sword. Of the pair on the right, the swordsman on the right has set aside his opponent's blow and finishes him off.

Plate 78

IV. POLE-AXE:[27] PLATES 79–103

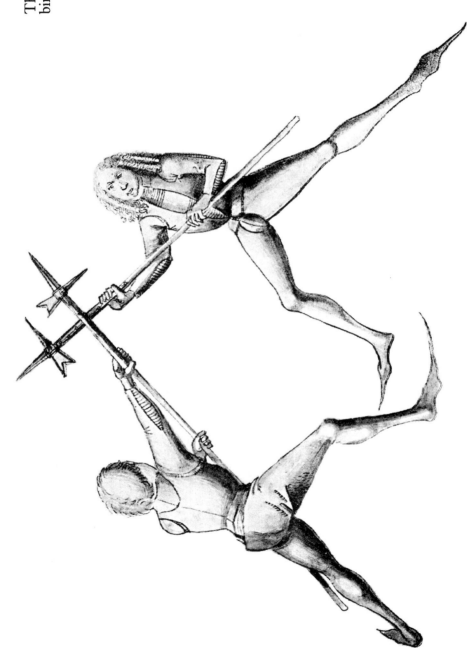

The two combatants
bind their pole-axes.

Plate 79

The combatant on the right disengages from the bind and thrusts to his opponent's belly with the butt of his pole-axe, rendering him defenceless.

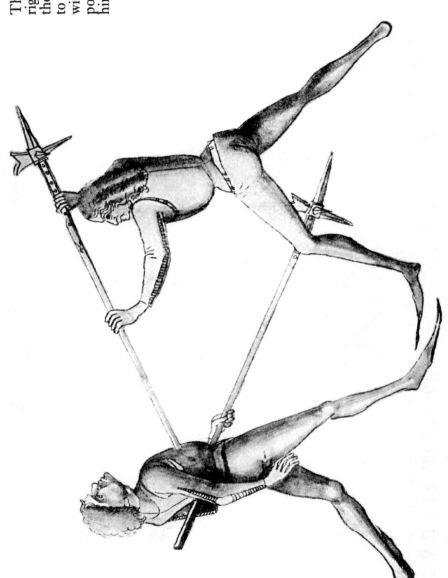

Plate 80

The combatant on the left prepares to strike from above. The combatant on the right trails his pole-axe behind himself, intending to set aside the oncoming blow and expose his opponent to a counter-attack.

Plate 81

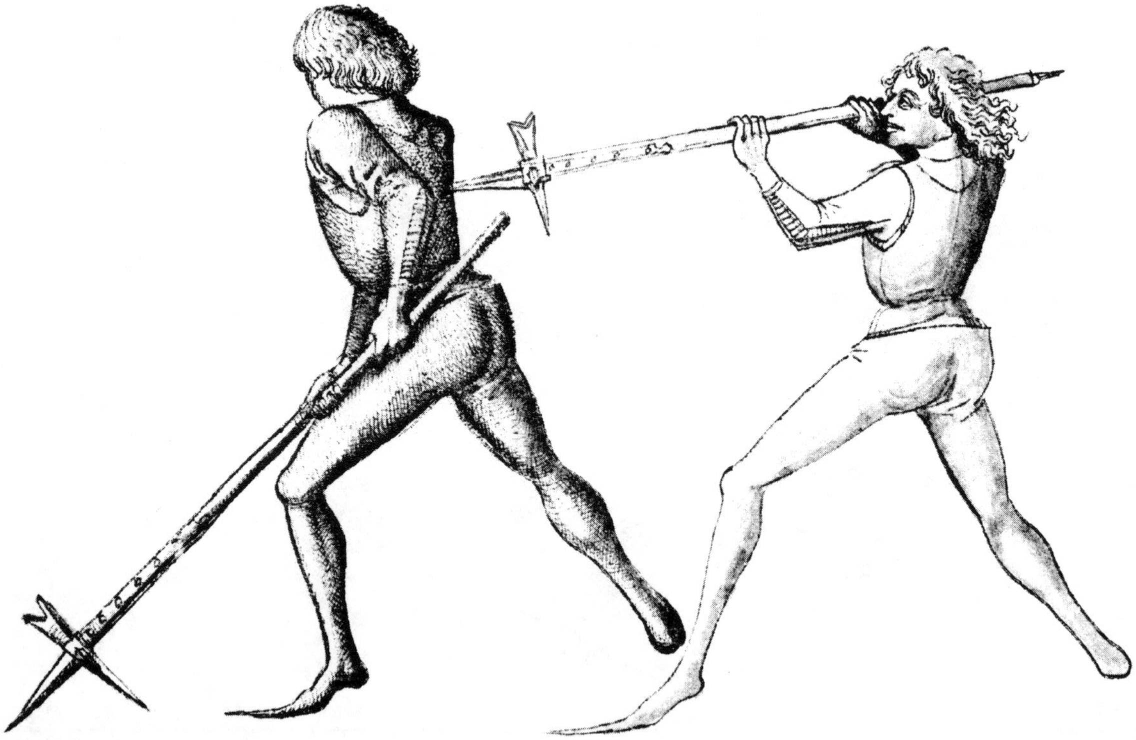

The combatant on the right sets aside his opponent's strike from above and completes his counter-attack by thrusting the top spike of his pole-axe into his enemy's flank.

Plate 82

The combatant on the left strikes with the false (back) edge. The combatant on the right sets aside the blow and wrenches his opponent behind the knee.

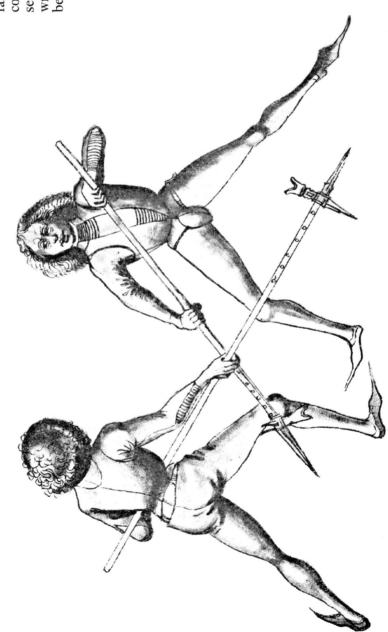

Plate 83

Both combatants strike from above and bind their pole-axes together. The fighter on the left quickly disengages, reverses his weapon and traps his opponent about the neck with the shaft.

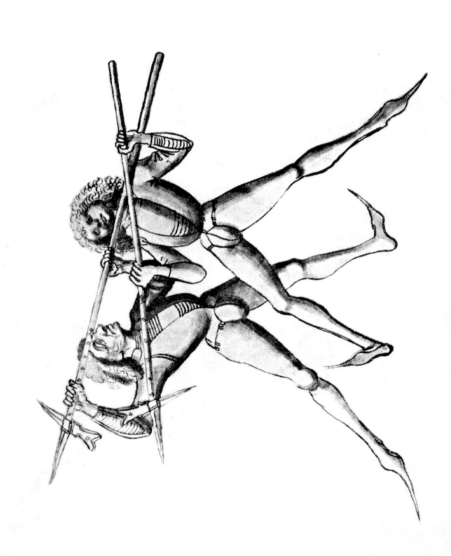

Plate 84

From the wrench, the combatant on the right steps forward and seizes his opponent about the neck and throws him over his hip.

Plate 85

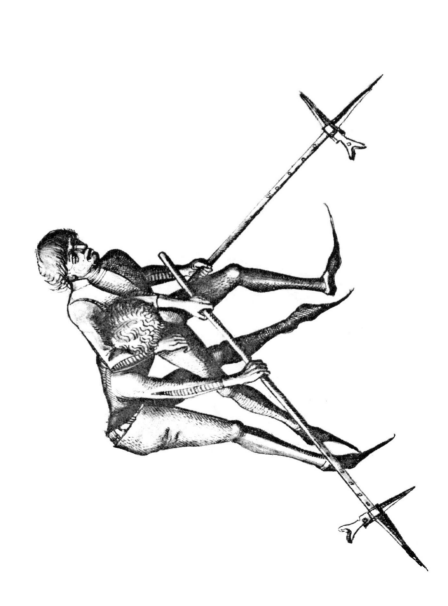

From a bind, the two combatants fall to the ground and wrestle. The combatant on top has his opponent in the 'knave hold', with his right arm around his enemy's throat and his right knee pressing into his enemy's belly.

Plate 86

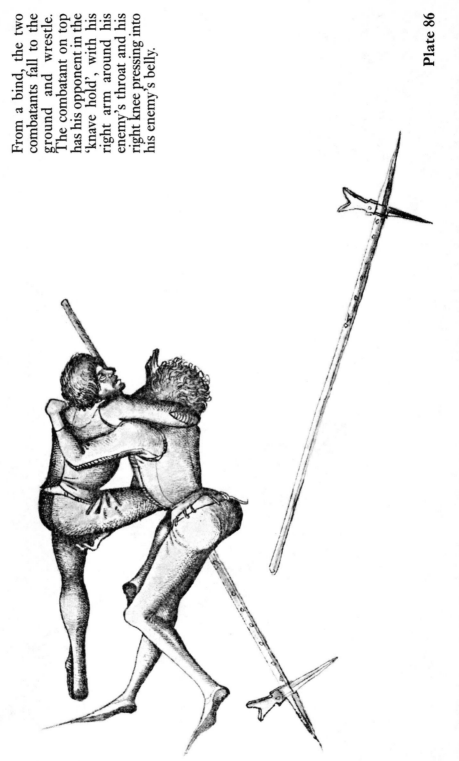

Plate 87

The combatant on the right strikes from above. The combatant on the left binds the pole-axes, discards his own weapon and closes with his opponent to grapple and throw him.

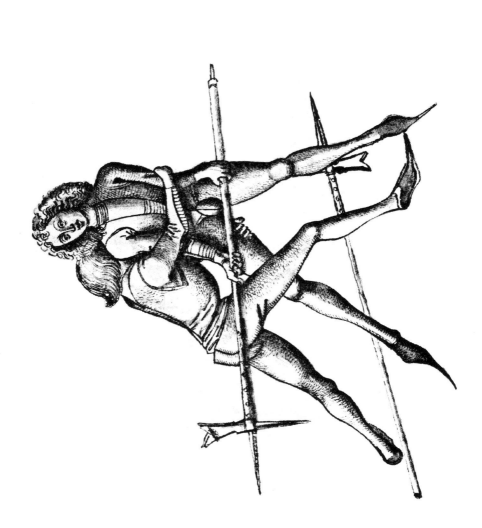

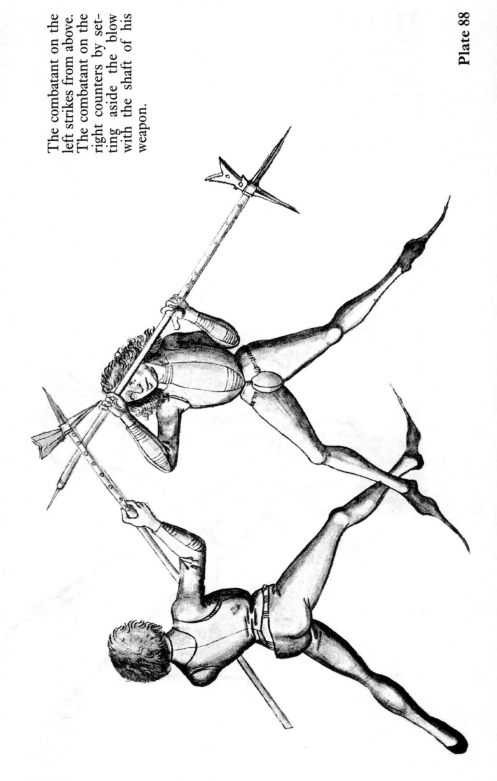

The combatant on the left strikes from above. The combatant on the right counters by setting aside the blow with the shaft of his weapon.

Plate 88

The combatant on the right steps forward and completes his counter-attack with a blow from above.

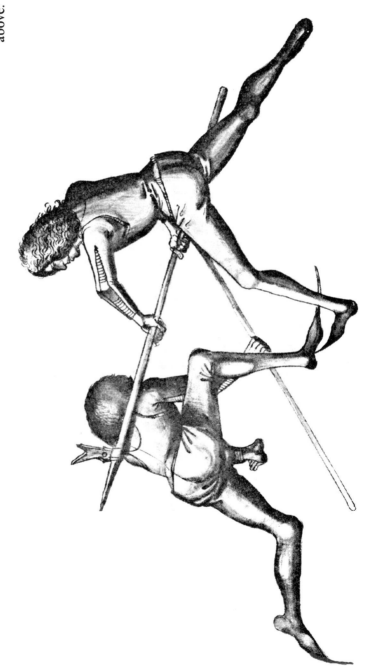

Plate 89

The combatant on the left strikes at his opponent's feet. The combatant on the right sets aside the blow with the shaft of his weapon and prepares to counterattack.

Plate 90

After setting aside the blow aimed at his feet, the combatant on the right strikes his opponent on the neck and hooks him with the spike of his pole-axe to wrench him to the ground.

Plate 91

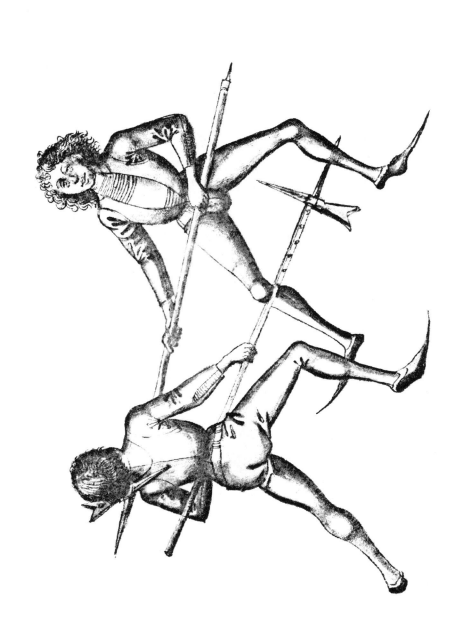

The combatant on the right thrusts at his opponent. The combatant on the left sets aside the thrust and hooks his enemy behind the neck to wrench him to the ground.

Plate 92

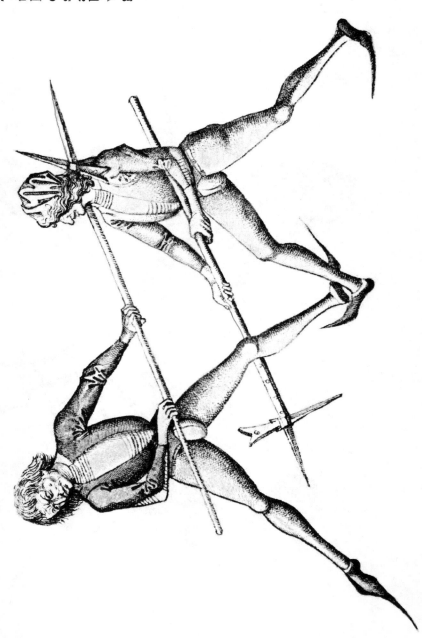

The combatant on the left counter-attacks by grappling for his opponent's weapon.

Plate 93

The combatant on the left finishes his counter-attack by grasping his opponent about the neck and throwing him over his thigh.

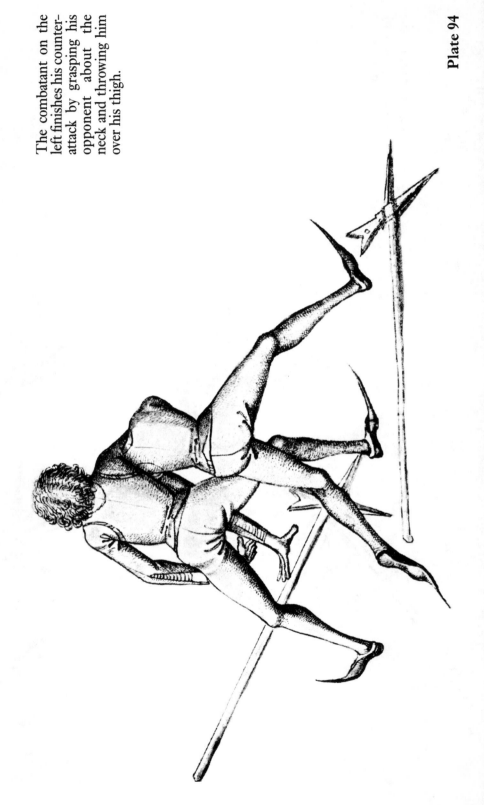

Plate 94

From a bind, the com-
batant on the right
traps his opponent
behind the elbow and
shoves him away.

Plate 95

The combatant on the left turns completely around to counter the attack described above.

Plate 96

The beginning of a new fight. The combatants are poised to threaten with both blows and thrusts.

Plate 97

The combatant on the left sets aside his opponent's thrust and is going to wrench him behind the knee.

Plate 98

A bind-behind.[28]

Plate 99

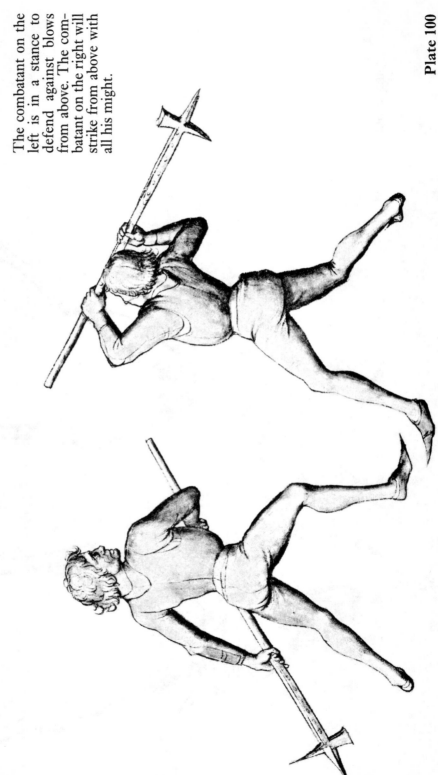

The combatant on the left is in a stance to defend against blows from above. The combatant on the right will strike from above with all his might.

Plate 100

The combatant on the left sets aside his opponent's stroke and thrusts into his belly.

Plate 101

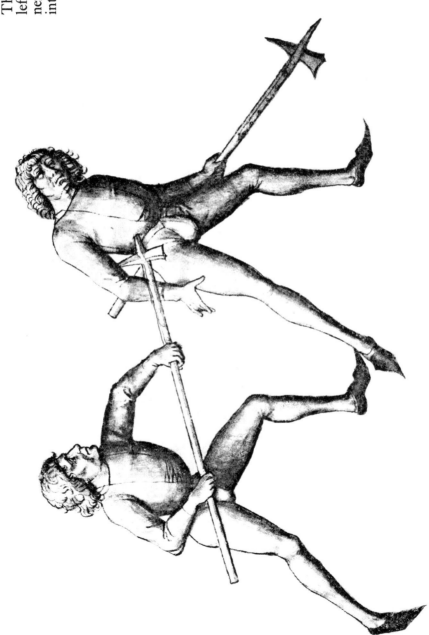

The combatant on the left tries to avoid his opponent's thrust. The combatant on the right thrusts at his opponent and strikes his pole-axe at his neck, hooking him to pull him onto his back.

Plate 102

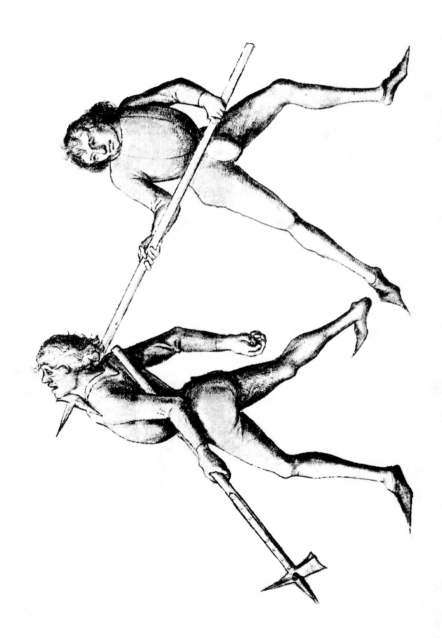

The combatant on top finishes off his opponent by stabbing him in the throat with his dagger.

Plate 103

V. SHIELD AND WOODEN MACE:[29] PLATES 104–26

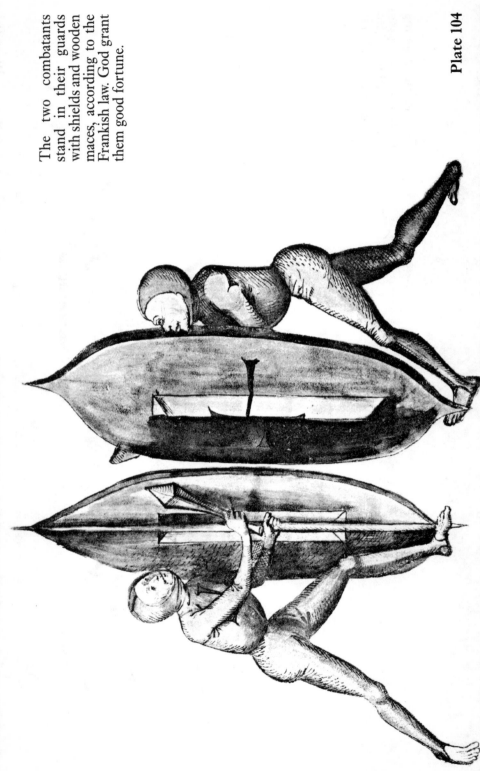

The two combatants stand in their guards with shields and wooden maces, according to the Frankish law. God grant them good fortune.

Plate 104

The combatant on the left is not afraid, knowing he can cover himself with his shield. The combatant on the right stands forth to the hazard.

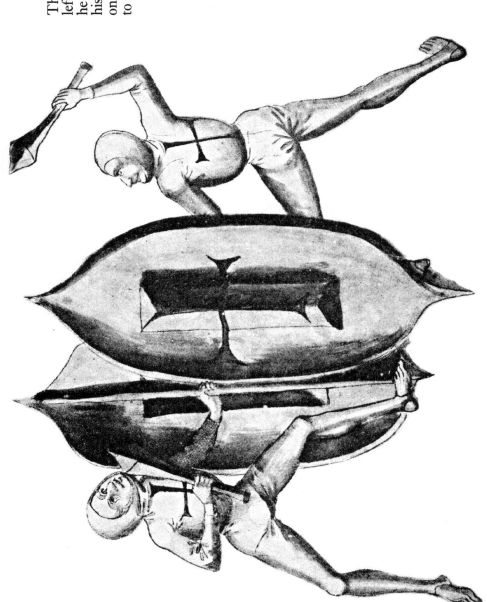

Plate 105

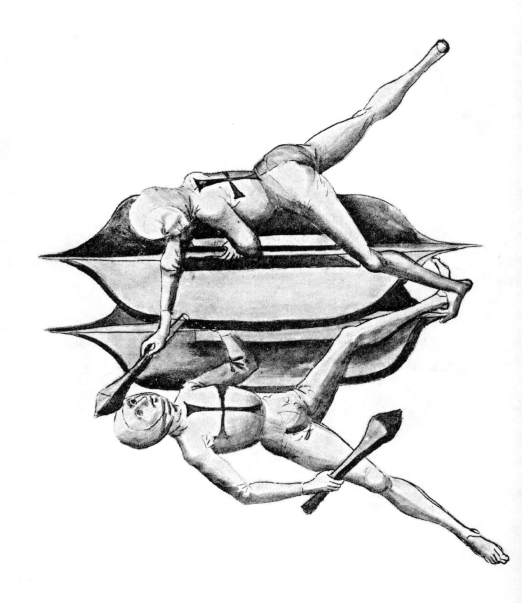

The combatant on the left is completely unprotected. The combatant on the right has interlocked his opponent's shield with his own and strikes at his head with his mace.

Plate 106

The combatant on the left is going to hammer his opponent with his shield. The combatant on the right prepares to step from behind his shield to strike his opponent on the head with his mace.

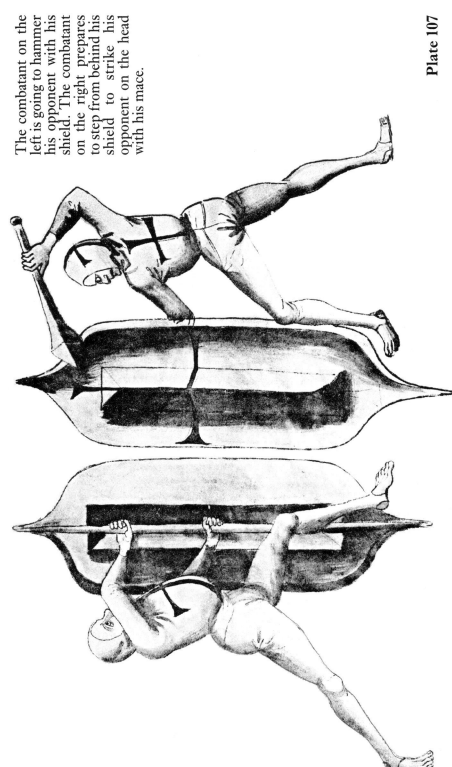

Plate 107

The combatant on the right binds his opponent's shield to create an opening. The combatant on the left is exposed to attack and fears a thrust with the shield-spike.

Plate 108

The combatant on the right finishes his opponent off with a thrust to the belly with his shield spike.

Plate 109

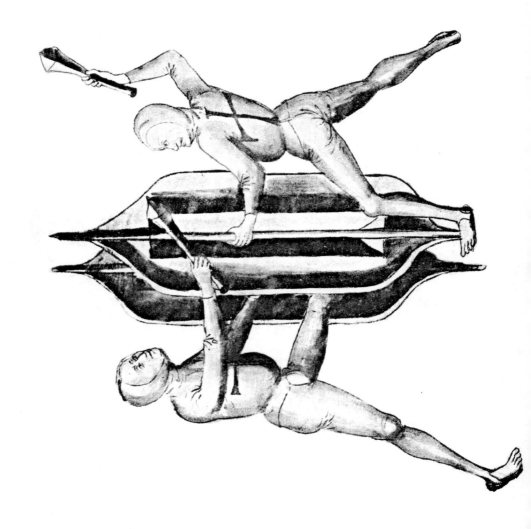

The combatant on the left kicks his opponent's shield, pivoting it to create an opening for attack. The combatant on the right prepares to throw his mace in defence.

Plate 110

The combatant on the left thrusts from above with his shield. The combatant on the right is going to bind his opponent's shield to find an opening near his enemy's heart.

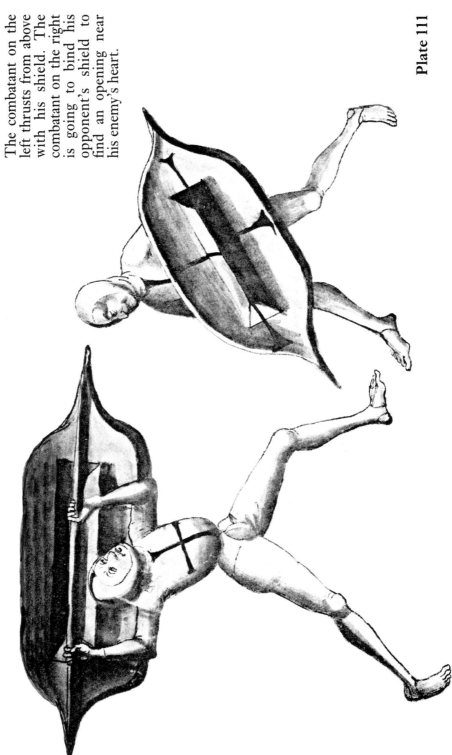

Plate 111

The attack described previously is completed.

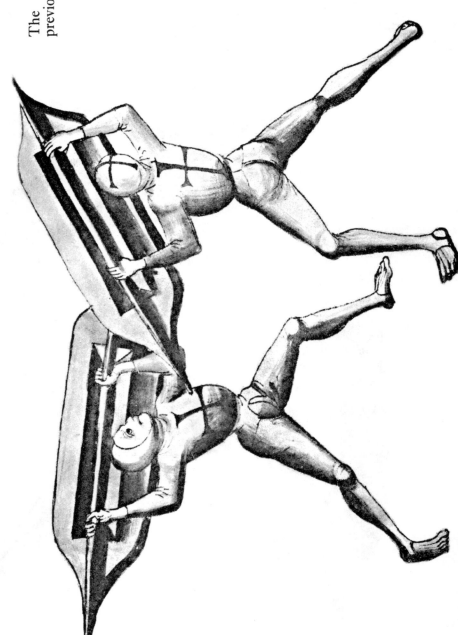

Plate 112

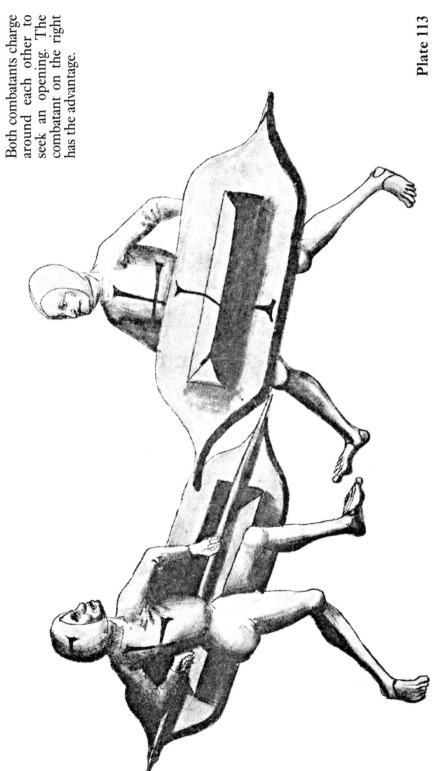

Both combatants charge around each other to seek an opening. The combatant on the right has the advantage.

Plate 113

The combatant on the left strikes his opponent's shield from one of his hands and looks for an opening into which to thrust. The combatant on the right defends himself by trapping and setting aside his opponent's shield with his arm.

Plate 114

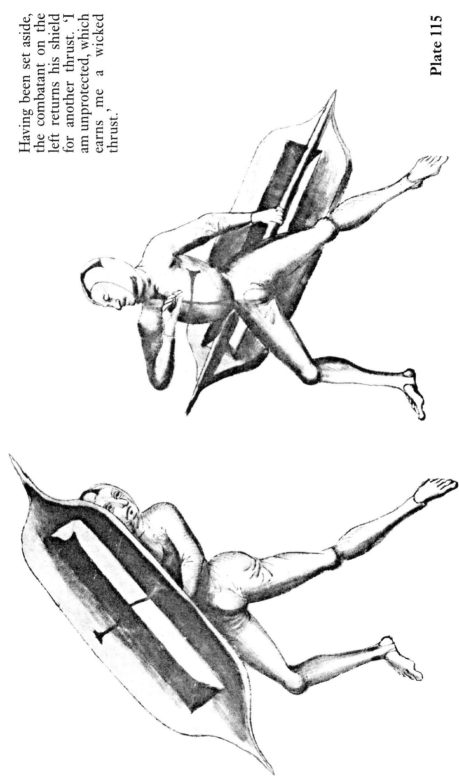

Having been set aside, the combatant on the left returns his shield for another thrust. 'I am unprotected, which earns me a wicked thrust.'

Plate 115

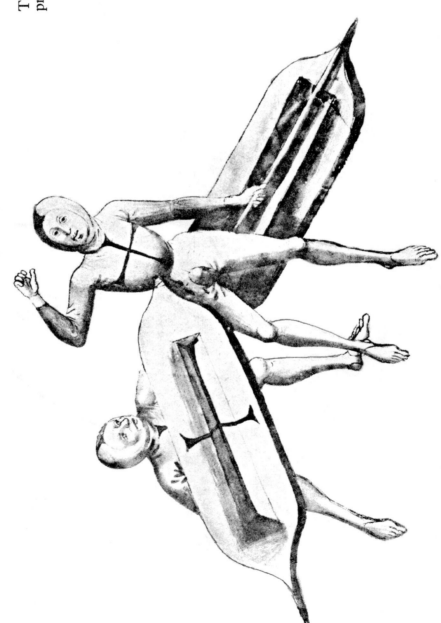

The attack described previously is completed.

Plate 116

The combatants bind
their shields again.

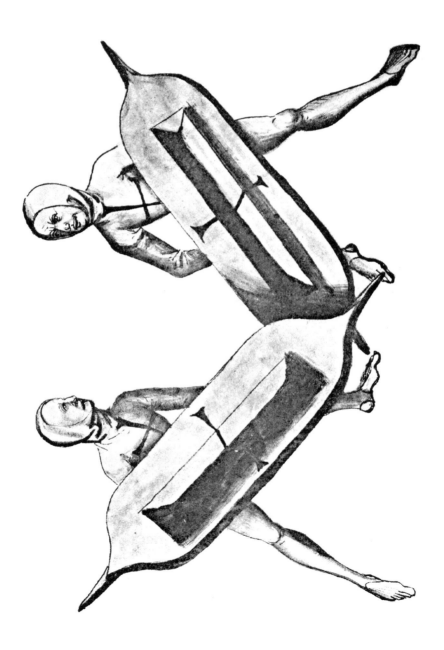

Plate 117

From the bind, the combatant on the left disengages his shield, pivots and thrusts his opponent in the thigh with his shield-spike.

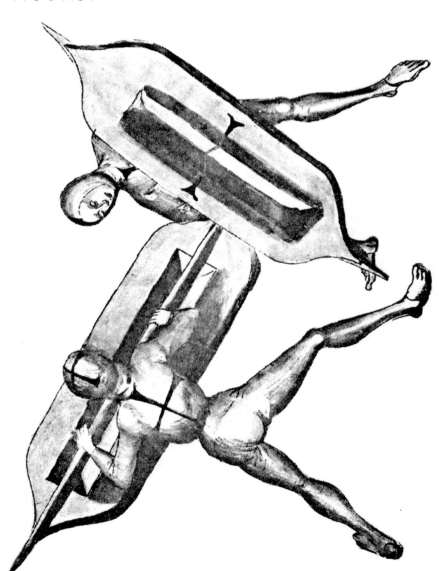

Plate 118

The combatant on the left awaits his opponent in a strong guard. The combatant on the right chops into his adversary's shield with his own to pull it behind himself.

Plate 119

The combatant on the left pulls his opponent's shield behind himself, as described above.

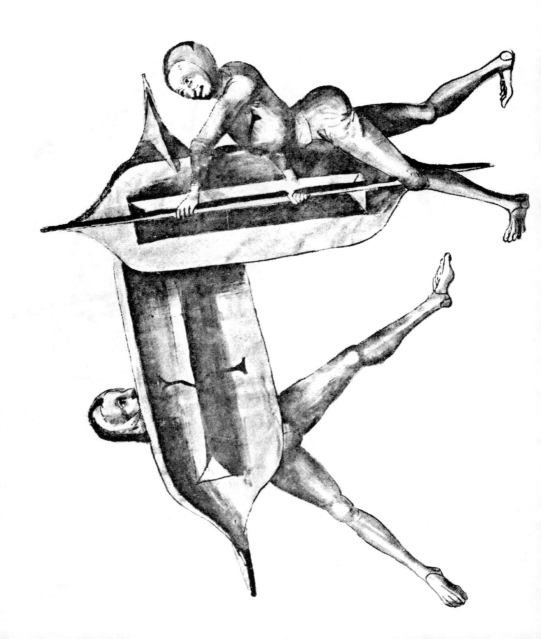

Plate 120

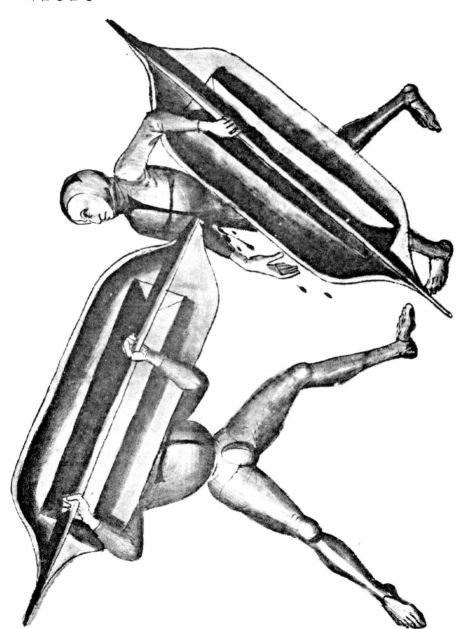

After pulling his opponent's shield away, the combatant on the left thrusts in behind it, completing the attack.

Plate 121

The combatant on the right pivots his shield, locking it with that of his opponent, and strikes at his adversary's head with his mace. The combatant on the left throws his right arm out, grasping over his opponent's right arm, and should now drop his shield, step forward, strike his adversary about the throat with his left arm, and throw him over his hip.

Plate 122

The attack described
above is completed.

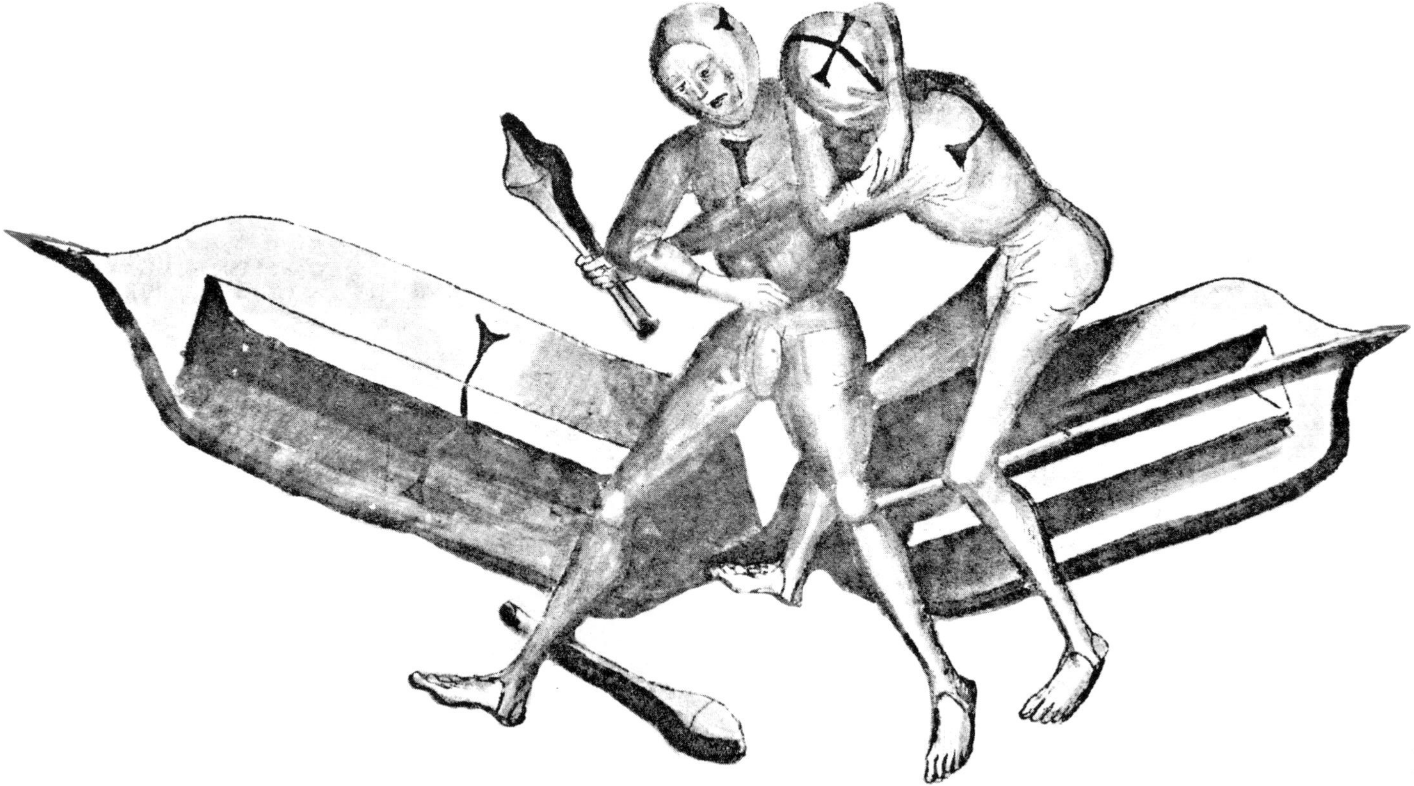

Plate 123

The combatant on the right strikes his shield between his opponent's shield and then releases it to throw his adversary. The combatant on the left is completely defenceless and gets thrown.

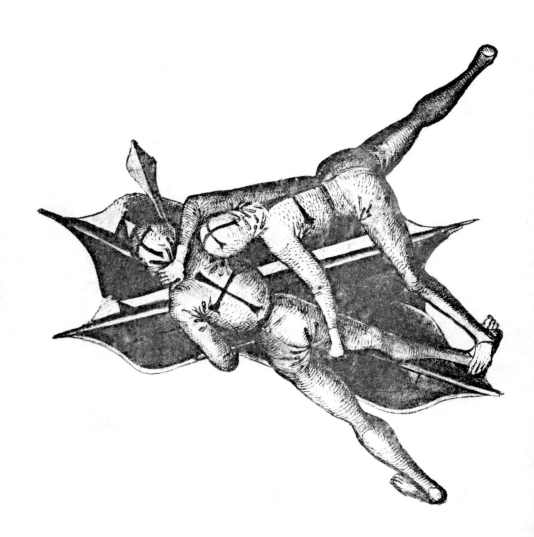

Plate 124

The combatant on top completes the throw and dispatches his opponent with a blow of his mace.

Plate 125

The combatants come away from their shields to strike each other with their maces. The combatant on the left sets aside his opponent's blow, grasps him by the arm, and strikes him to death. The combat with maces is at an end.

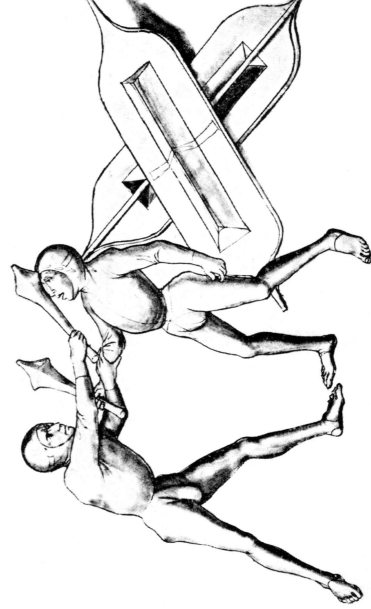

Plate 126

VI. SHIELD AND SWORD:[30] PLATES 128–50

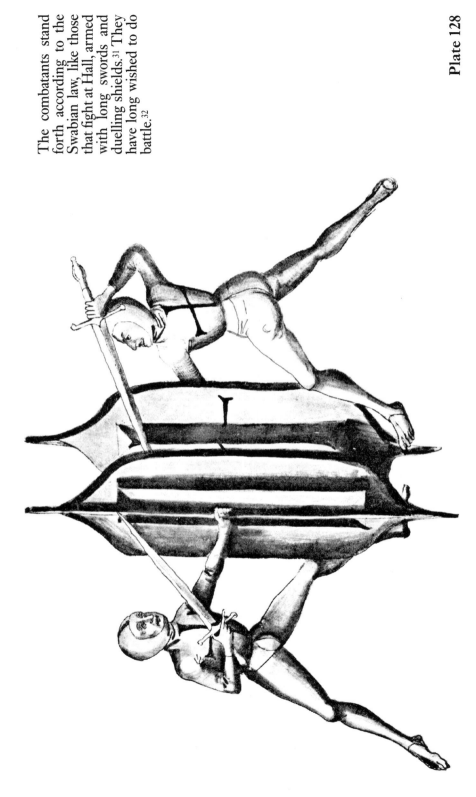

The combatants stand forth according to the Swabian law, like those that fight at Hall, armed with long swords and duelling shields.[31] They have long wished to do battle.[32]

Plate 128

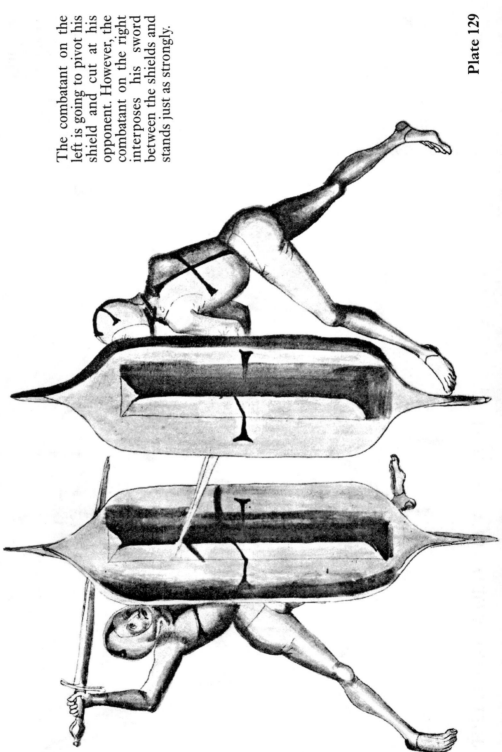

The combatant on the left is going to pivot his shield and cut at his opponent. However, the combatant on the right interposes his sword between the shields and stands just as strongly.

Plate 129

The combatant on the right stands with his body exposed. The combatant on the left thrusts crosswise (with his hand inverted) along the shields.

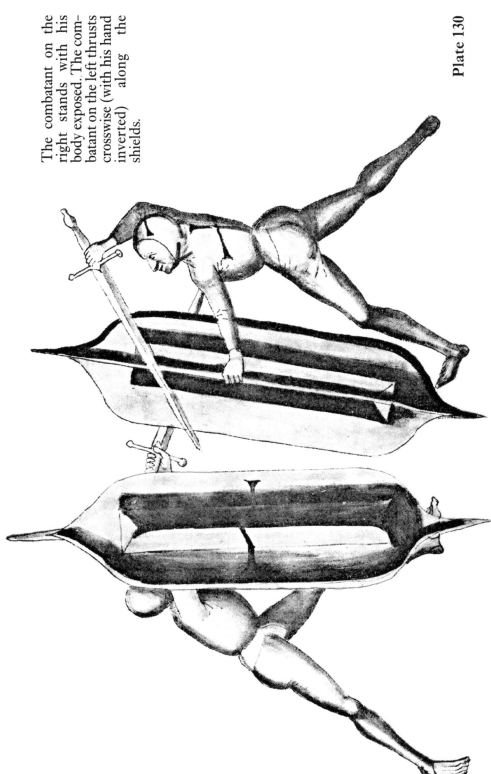

Plate 130

The same action as before viewed from the other side.

Plate 131

The combatant on the right has turned his shield completely around, leaving himself exposed. The combatant on the left hides behind his shield, then quickly pivots it and strides forward with a thrust below his opponent's arm.

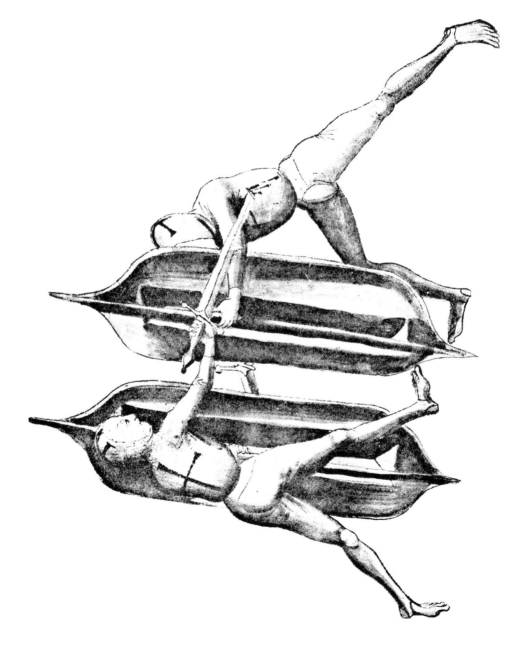

Plate 132

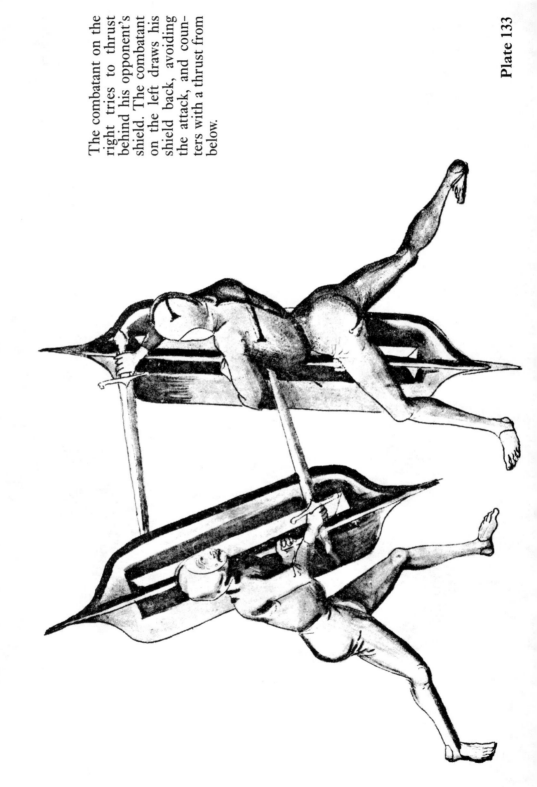

The combatant on the right tries to thrust behind his opponent's shield. The combatant on the left draws his shield back, avoiding the attack, and counters with a thrust from below.

Plate 133

The combatant on the left charges in, kicks his opponent's shield open and succeeds in thrusting him through.

Plate 134

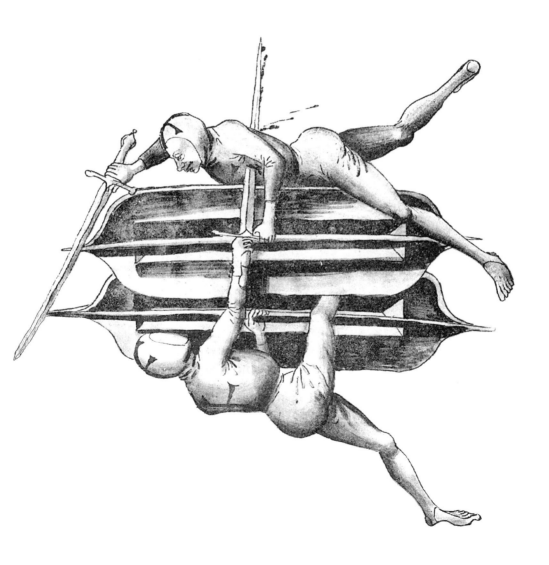

The combatant on the left sets aside his opponent's shield to prevent him from cutting and thrusting. Note how the shield of the combatant on the right is turned.

Plate 135

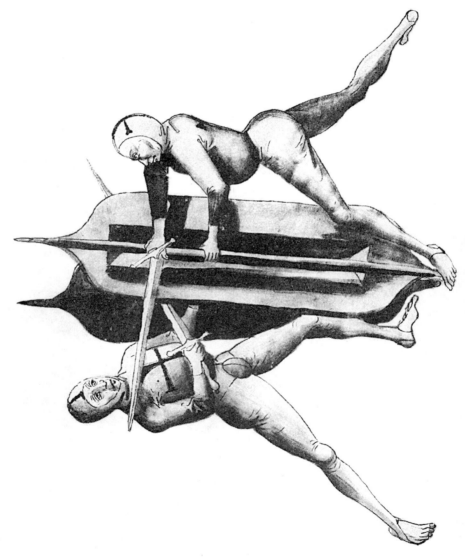

The combatant on the right tries to thrust between the shields. The combatant on the left drops his shield and cuts from above at his exposed opponent.

Plate 136

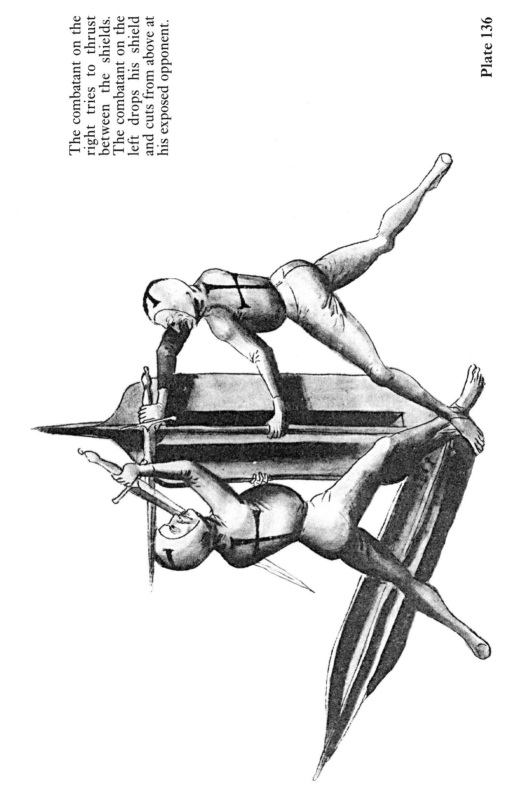

Plate 137

This, however, is how the fight ends: the combatant on the right drops his shield and grasps his opponent by the elbow, turns him around, and thrusts him through the neck.

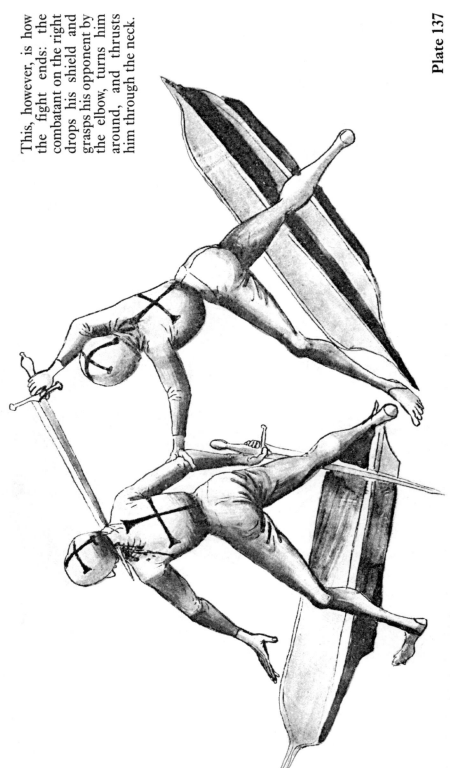

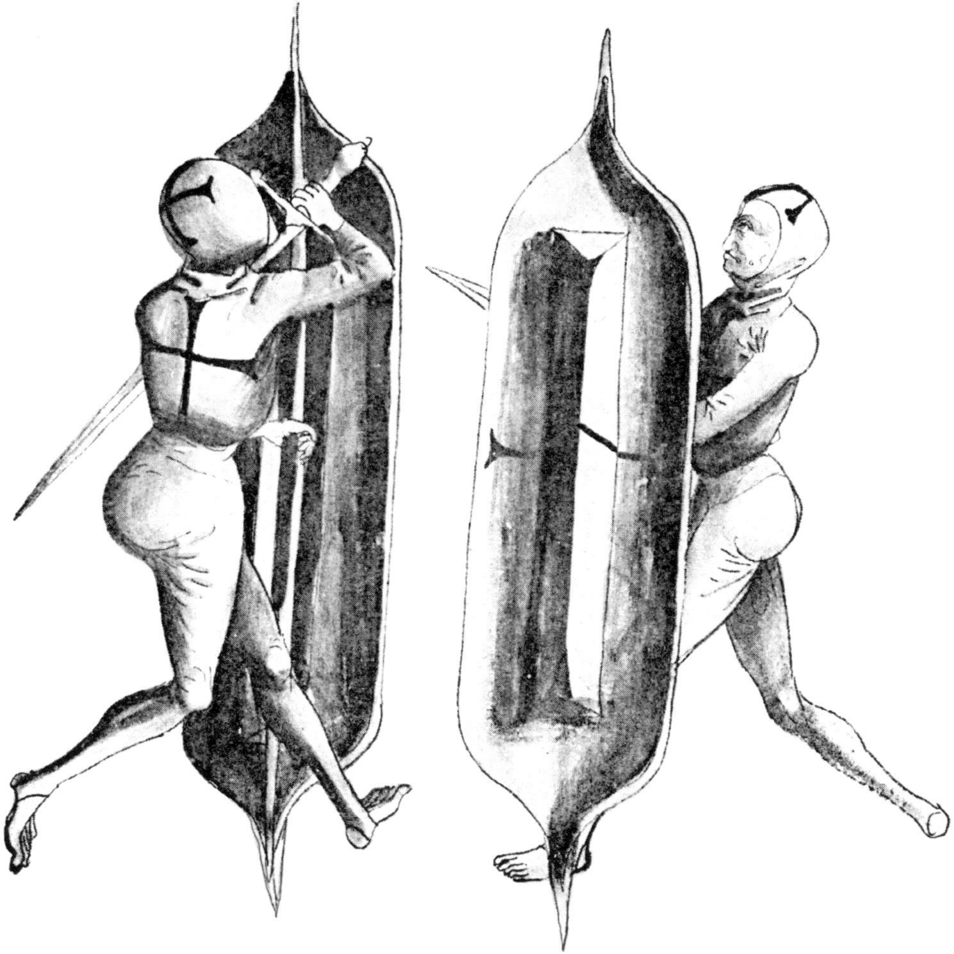

The combatant on the right stands in a strong guard. The combatant on the left moves in to hammer his opponent with both sword and shield to create an opening for attack.

Plate 138

The combatant on the right lures his opponent into a failed attack and then counters with a thrust to the neck. 'He really fooled me with that one!'

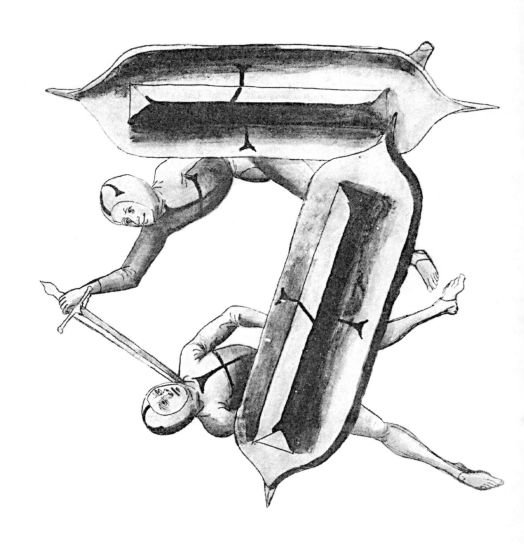

Plate 139

From a bind, the combatant on the right disengages, grasping his sword and shield together to thrust from above. The combatant on the left sees the thrust coming and prevents his adversary from bringing his shield around.

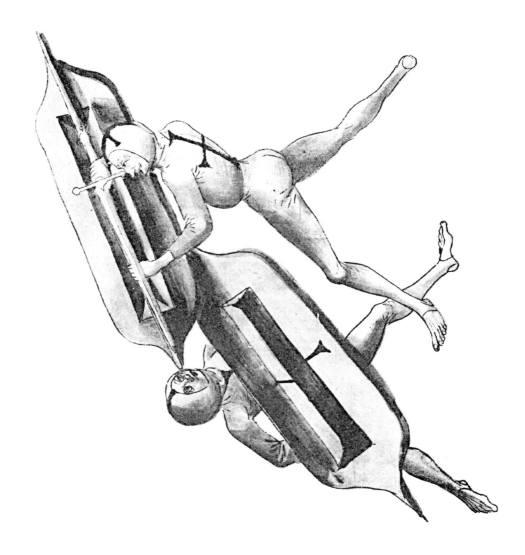

Plate 140

The combatant on the left cuts closely between the two shields, striking his opponent on the head. 'I tried to cut cross-wise and am undone!'[33]

Plate 141

The combatant on the left steps forward with a crosswise cut. Mark that the combatant on the right thrusts quickly through his opponent's thigh before the cut can land.

Plate 142

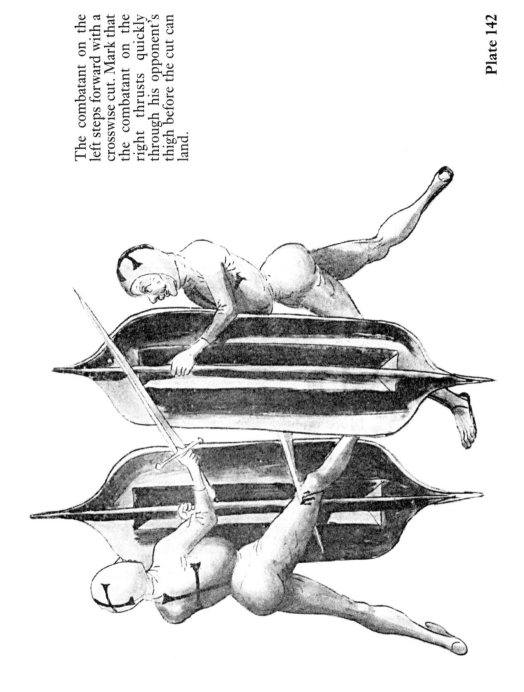

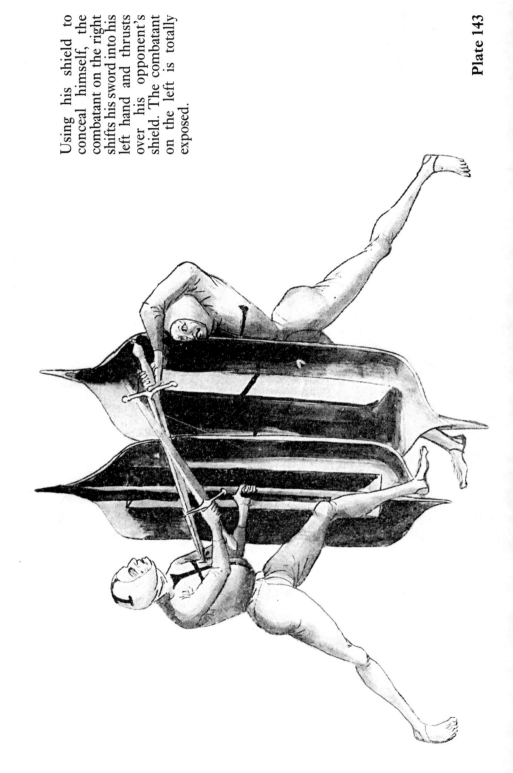

Using his shield to conceal himself, the combatant on the right shifts his sword into his left hand and thrusts over his opponent's shield. The combatant on the left is totally exposed.

Plate 143

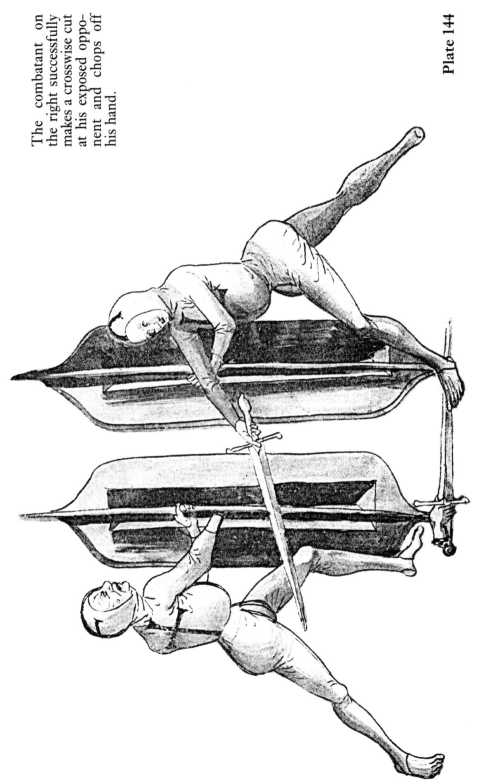

The combatant on the right successfully makes a crosswise cut at his exposed opponent and chops off his hand.

Plate 144

The combatant on the left is in the same stance as the fellow above who lost his hand. The combatant on the right is going to attack over his shield if he finds his opponent exposed.

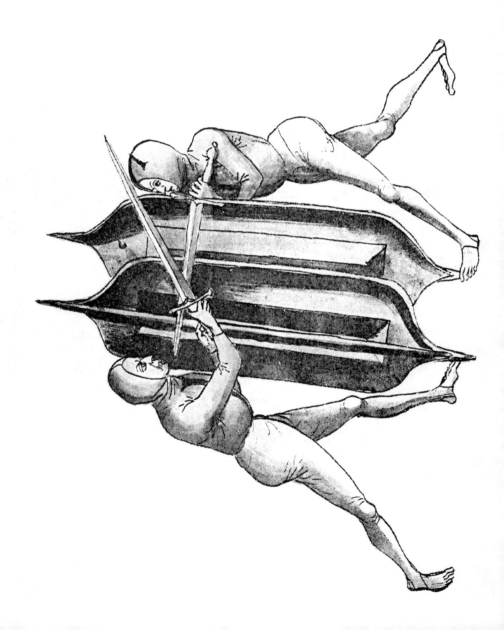

Plate 145

Both combatants stand unprotected. The combatant on the right can throw his shield at his opponent to force him away.

Plate 146

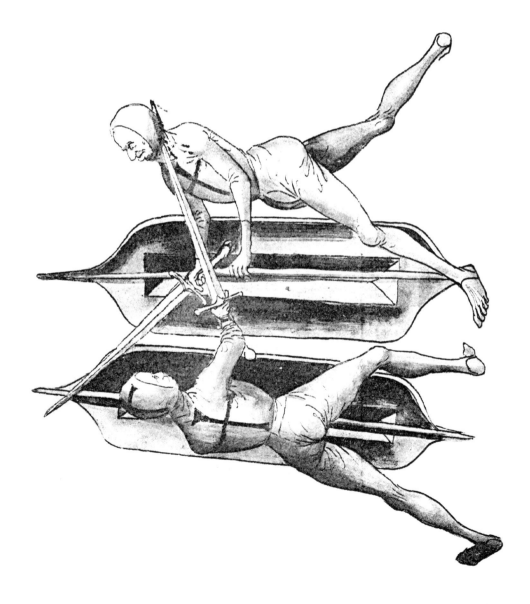

The combatant on the right throws his shield at his opponent and shoves him away, forcing him to crouch, so he may hew him upon his head and back.

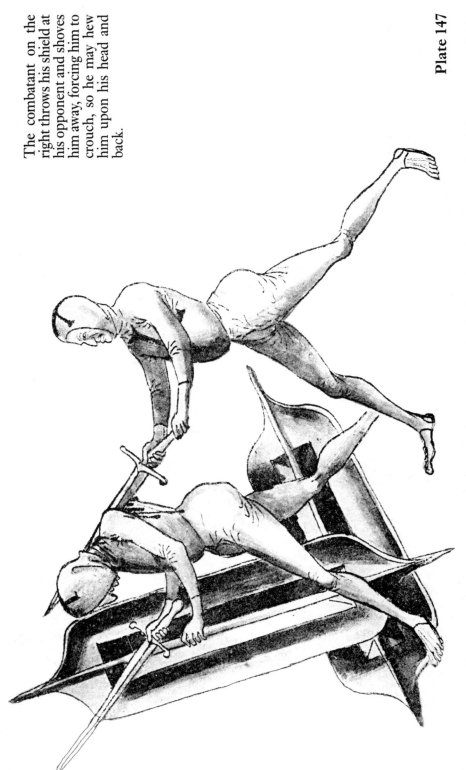

Plate 147

The combatant on the left tries to bind and wrench his opponent with his sword and shield together. The combatant on the right counters by moving back, shrugging off the attack, dropping his shield, and stepping forth to hew his opponent upon the back of the neck.

Plate 148

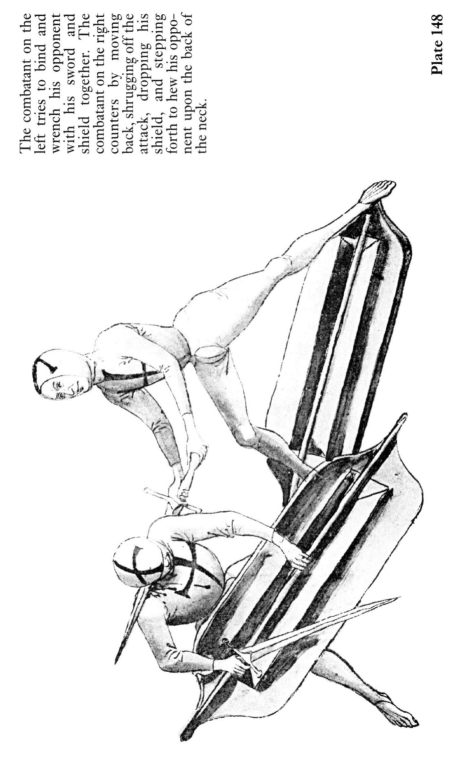

The combatant on the left angles his shield in from above. The combatant on the right should be able to see the inside of his opponent's shield and ought to thrust crosswise.

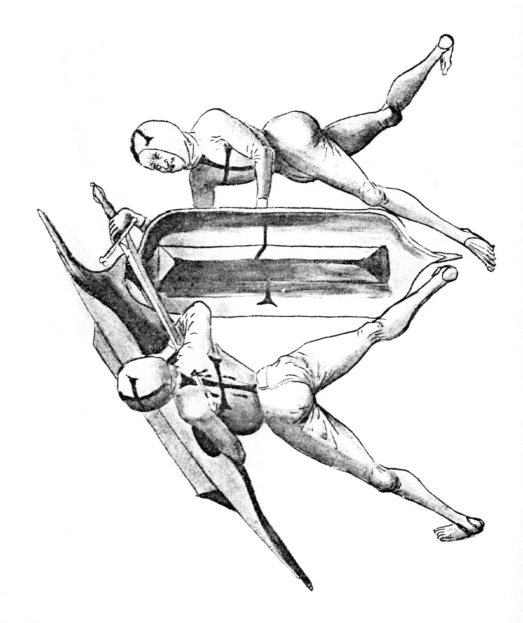

Plate 149

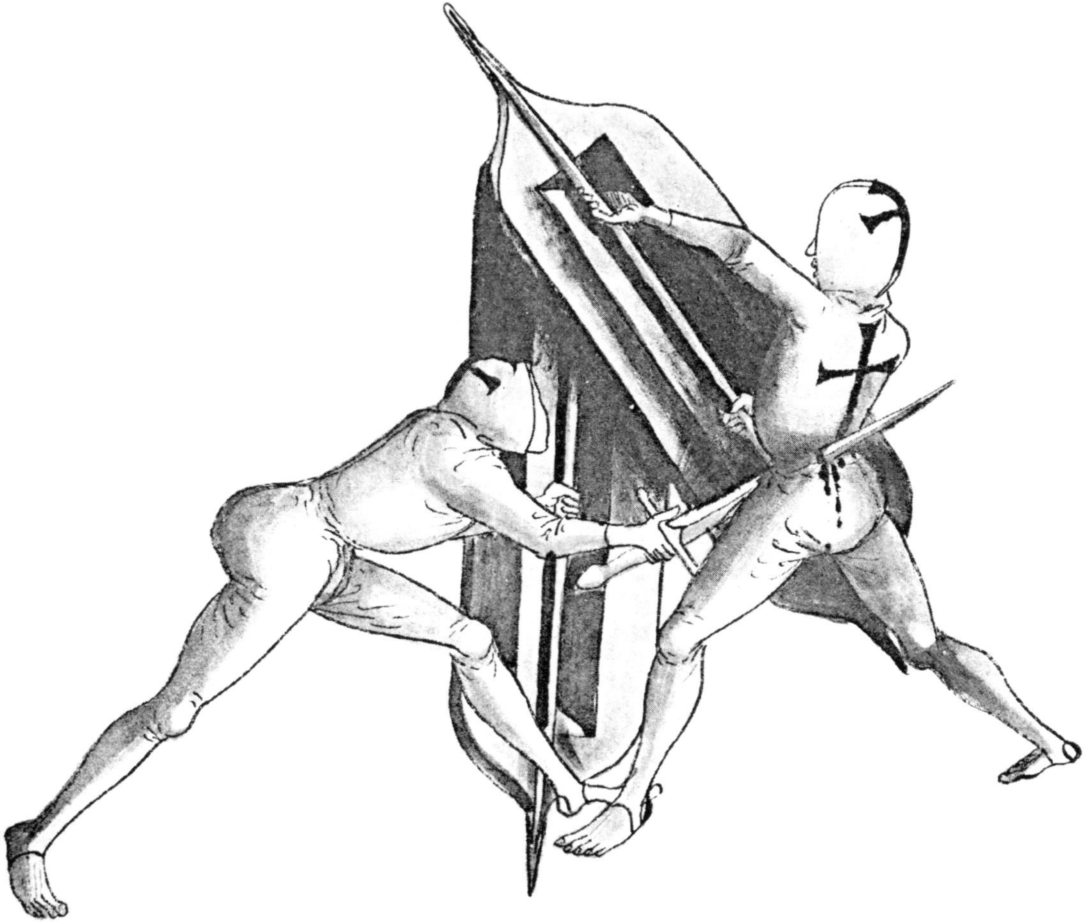

The combatant on the right hammers at his opponent with his shield in order to disarm him. The combatant on the left remains standing and is able to counter by thrusting through his opponent from below.

Plate 150

The combatant on the right strikes his opponent with his shield. The combatant on the left counters by grasping his opponent about the neck and throwing him and his shield.

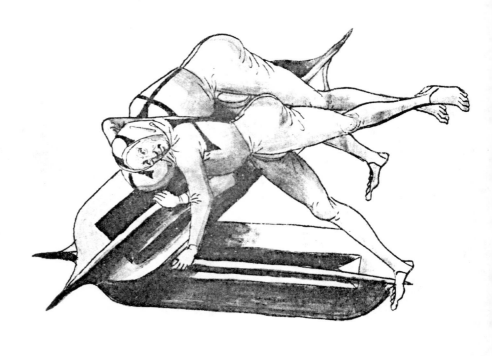

Plate 151

The attack described above is completed.

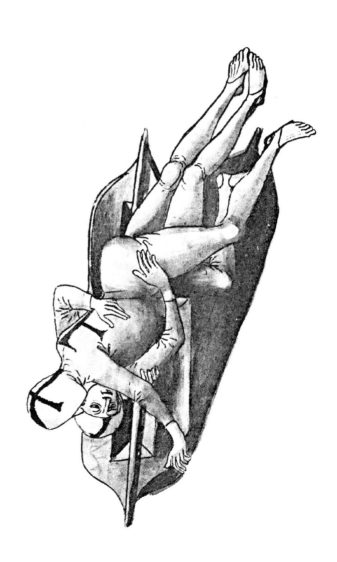

Plate 152

The combatant on the left binds his shield between his opponent's shield, and hooks behind his adversary's foot to wrench him.[35] The combatant on the right realizes too late what is happening and must suffer the consequences.

Plate 153

From a bind, one may wrench either high or low on either side.

Plate 154

Going high is as good as going low. However, from the high bind of the combatant on the right, his opponent may grasp the point of the shield and wrench it away from him.

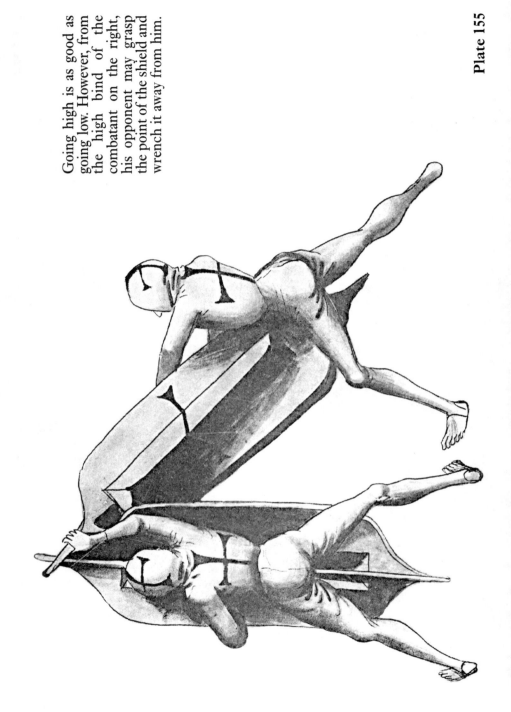

Plate 155

From the action described above, if the combatant doesn't let go of his shield, it must lead to wrestling.

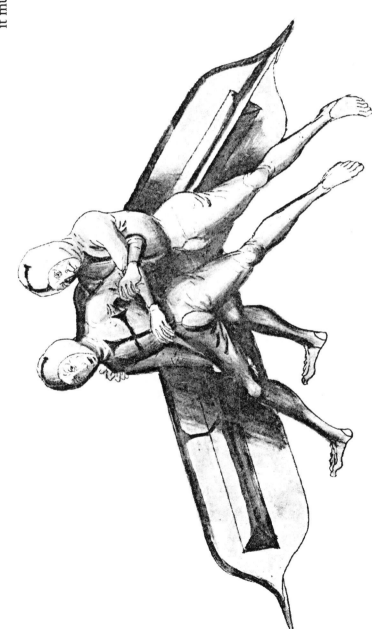

Plate 156

Mark the correct way to attack. The combatant on the right hammers in with his shield to expose his opponent. The combatant on the left stands firmly and lets go of his shield with his right hand and grasps his opponent by the elbow and shoves him away from himself, turning him around.

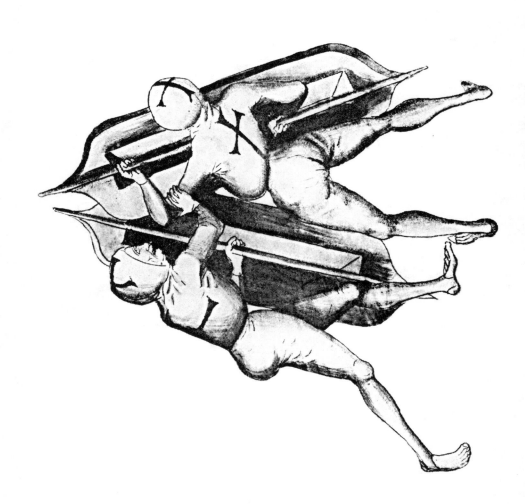

Plate 157

The combatant on the left thrusts his opponent away by the elbow, as described above. However, the combatant on the right turns all the way around and thrusts his shield-spike into his adversary, completing the attack and counter.

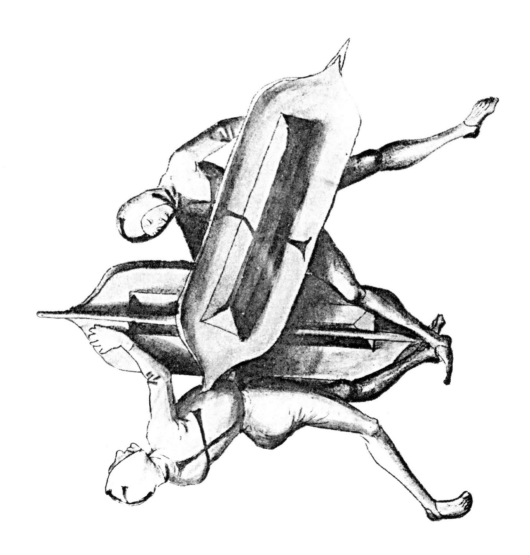

Plate 158

The combatant on the left charges in and steps behind his opponent, engaging him in a high guard. He must beware of being thrown. The combatant on the right receives the charge and must throw his adversary or disarm him.

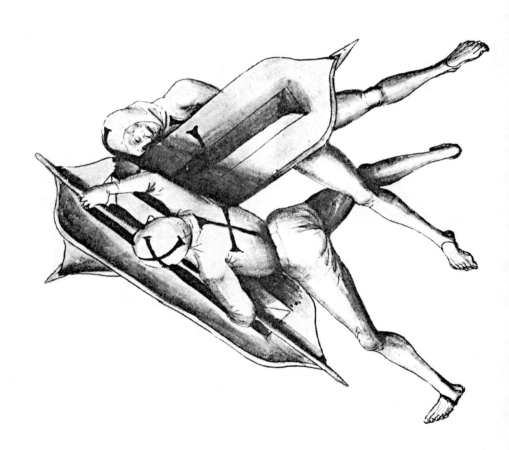

Plate 159

The combatant previously on the right, now on the left, counters his opponent with a throw, as described above. He finishes him off with a thrust to the throat with his shield-spike.

Plate 160

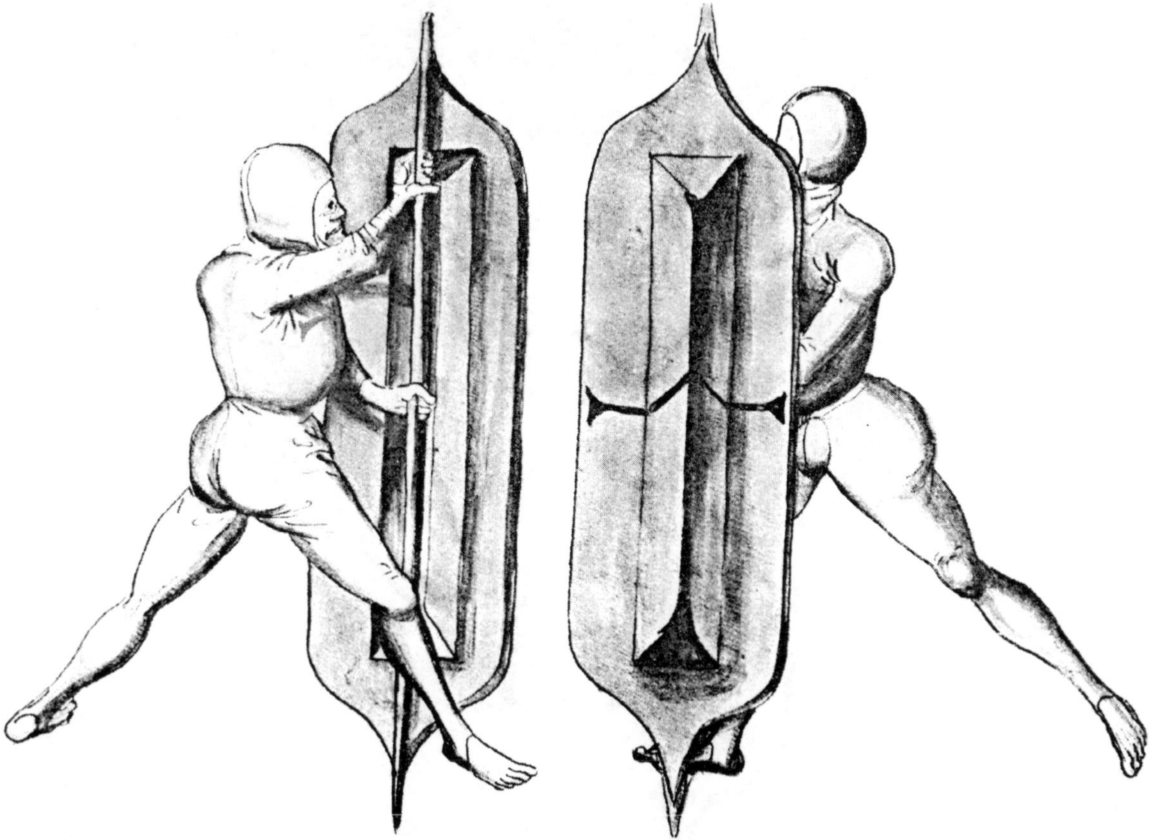

Both combatants stand in their guards, ready to strike with the inverted bind.[36]

Plate 161

The combatant on the left offers the weak part of his shield to the strong part of his opponent's shield.[37] Mark his struggle closely. Each combatant wants to free himself from the bind, so that he may attack his opponent behind his shield and disarm him.

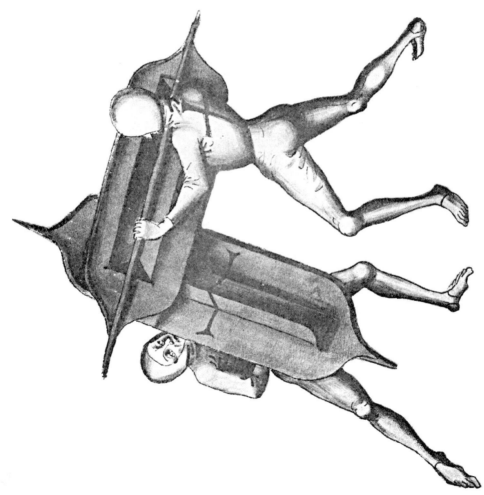

Plate 162

The combatant on the left gets the strong of his shield upon the weak of his opponent's shield and may thrust at him or wrench him. The combatant on the right has lost his strong (his ability to create leverage) and will be pulled down.

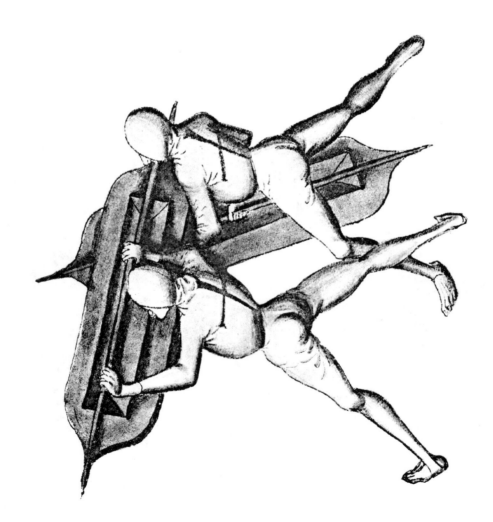

Plate 163

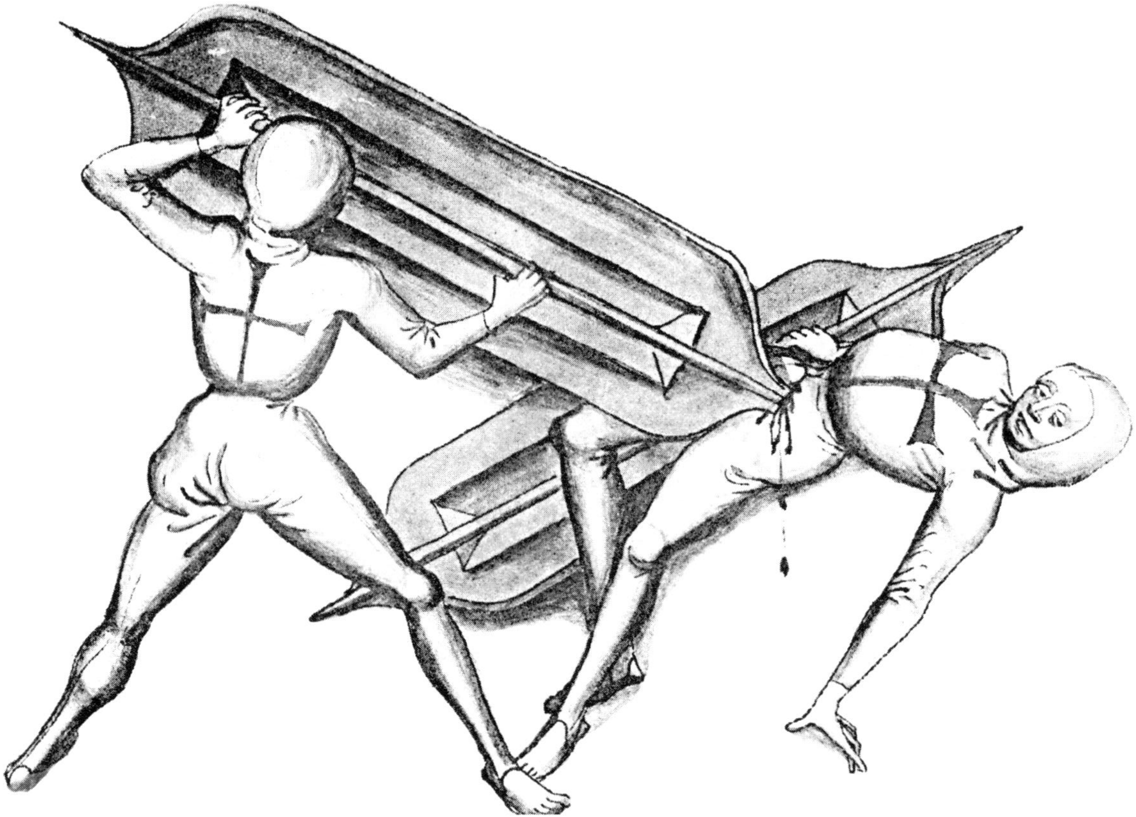

The combatant on the left finishes off his opponent by thrusting him in the groin with his shield-spike.

Plate 164

VIII. THROATED HOOKING SHIELD:[38] PLATES 165–9

The combatant on the left deliberately exposes himself to attack and thrusts below the weak part of his opponent's shield to hook his adversary's foot and wrench it. This gambit is dangerous, however, because the combatant on the right can still attack from above.

Plate 165

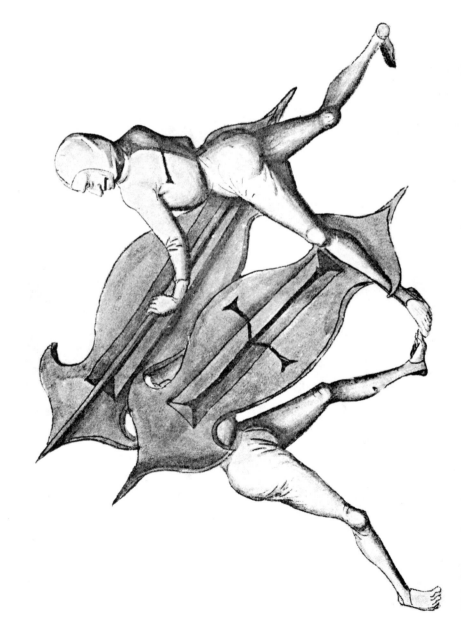

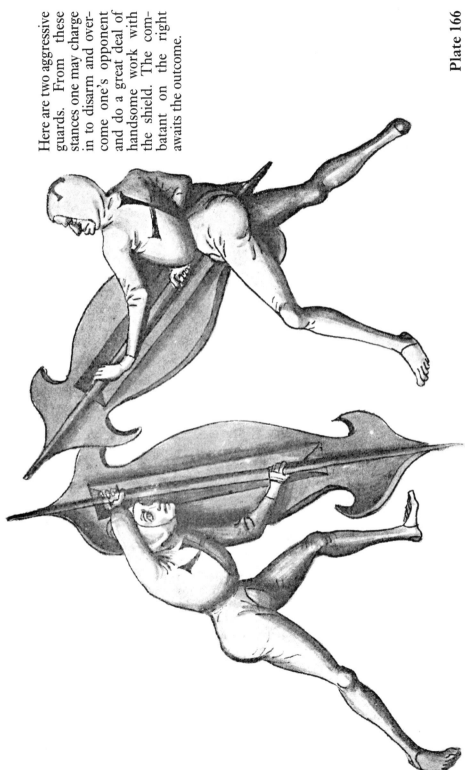

Here are two aggressive guards. From these stances one may charge in to disarm and overcome one's opponent and do a great deal of handsome work with the shield. The combatant on the right awaits the outcome.

Plate 166

The combatant on the left has deflected his opponent's blow and thrusts up into his shield to strike at his neck. The combatant on the right tries to bind the shields. Go to the next page to see the completed attack.

Plate 167

The combatant on the right disengages and spins his shield to hook his opponent behind the neck and drag him to the ground, completing the attack described above.

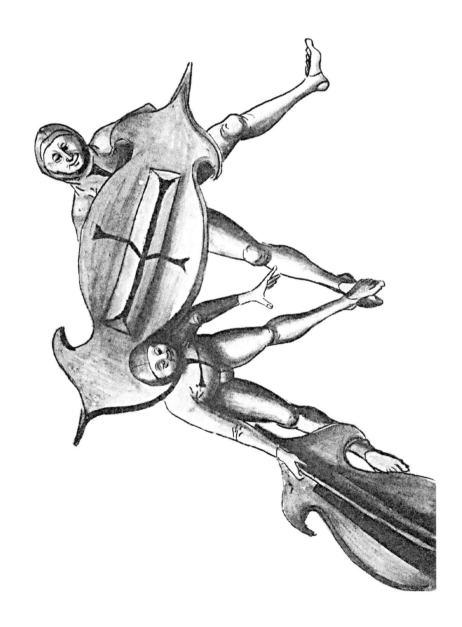

Plate 168

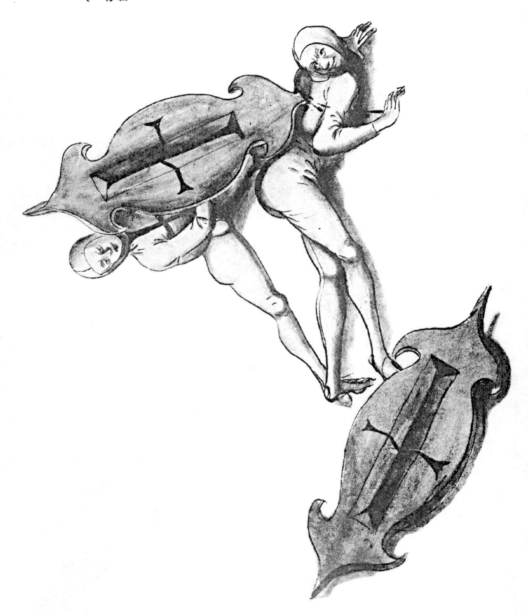

The shield fight is at an end. God deliver us from all worry.

Plate 169

IX. DAGGER:³⁹ PLATES 170–89

Now we take up the dagger. God preserve us all! From left to right: the first fighter stabs from above. The second fighter sets aside the stab and turns the dagger away from himself (trapping his opponent's dagger and twisting it out of his hand). The third fighter stabs from above. The fourth fighter thrusts from below to set aside the blow and counter it.

Plate 170

The fighter on the far left makes the upper shield with his dagger to block his opponent's stab from above.[40] The fighter on the far right stabs from below and his opponent makes the lower shield to block the stab.

Plate 171

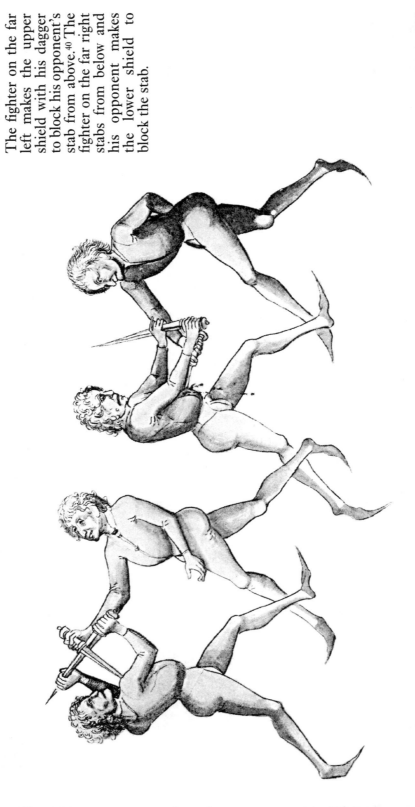

As the fighter second from the left stabs from above, his opponent counters by throwing out his left arm to catch the stab and then strikes or slashes with his own dagger. The fighter on the far right stabs from above. His opponent surprises him and counters by catching the stab with the left arm, twisting it around his own dagger arm, and then throwing his attacker away from himself.

Plate 172

The fighter on the far left counters his opponent's stab from above by catching the stab with his left arm, seizing him with his dagger between the legs and drawing him upward to throw him away from himself. The fighter second from the right counters his opponent's stab from above by setting it aside with his right arm and wringing his own dagger around his attacker's arm to trap him and throw him away from himself.

Plate 173

The fighter on the far left was entangled by his opponent, but countered by stepping out and reversing the hold. The fighter on the far right stabs from above. His opponent entangles him with the scissors-hold.[41]

Plate 174

To counter his opponent's stab from above, the fighter on the far left catches the stab with his right arm, twists it down, traps his opponent's right arm with his left arm, pivots and throws his opponent to the ground. On the right, the counter and throw are completed.

Plate 175

As soon as his opponent stabs from above, the fighter second from the left moves his right arm against the stab, grasps his opponent's right arm with his left hand upon the elbow and presses him away. However, as shown with the pair on the right, his opponent can pivot, get a grip beneath his leg, and throw him over onto his back.

Plate 176

The fighter on the far left sets aside his opponent's stab from above with his right arm and counter-thrusts into his attacker's belly. The fighter second from the right has put his adversary in the scissors-hold, and should now attack either the arm or the throat.

Plate 177

The fighter on the far left counters the stab from above by trapping the stab with his left arm and grasping with his right hand under his opponent's right arm to throw him backwards. The fighter second from the right traps his opponent's stab from above with his right arm, pivots, throws his left arm around his opponent's neck and throws him over his hip.

Plate 178

The fighter on the far left counters the stab from above by catching and trapping it with his right arm and grasping his opponent's dagger arm at the elbow with his left hand and pressing down on the elbow. In the pair on the right we see the counter-move: the attacker turns completely around and throws the defender over his hip.

Plate 179

The fighter on the far left counters a thrust from below by striking his opponent's thrusting arm with his right fist and thrusting into his adversary's belly. The pair on the right are at an impasse.

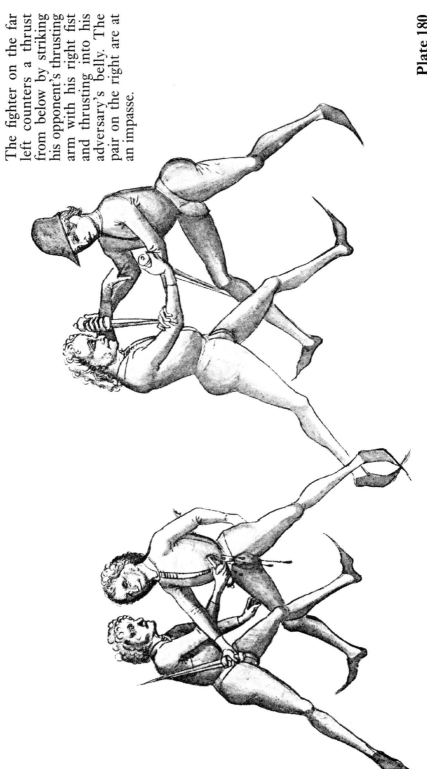

Plate 180

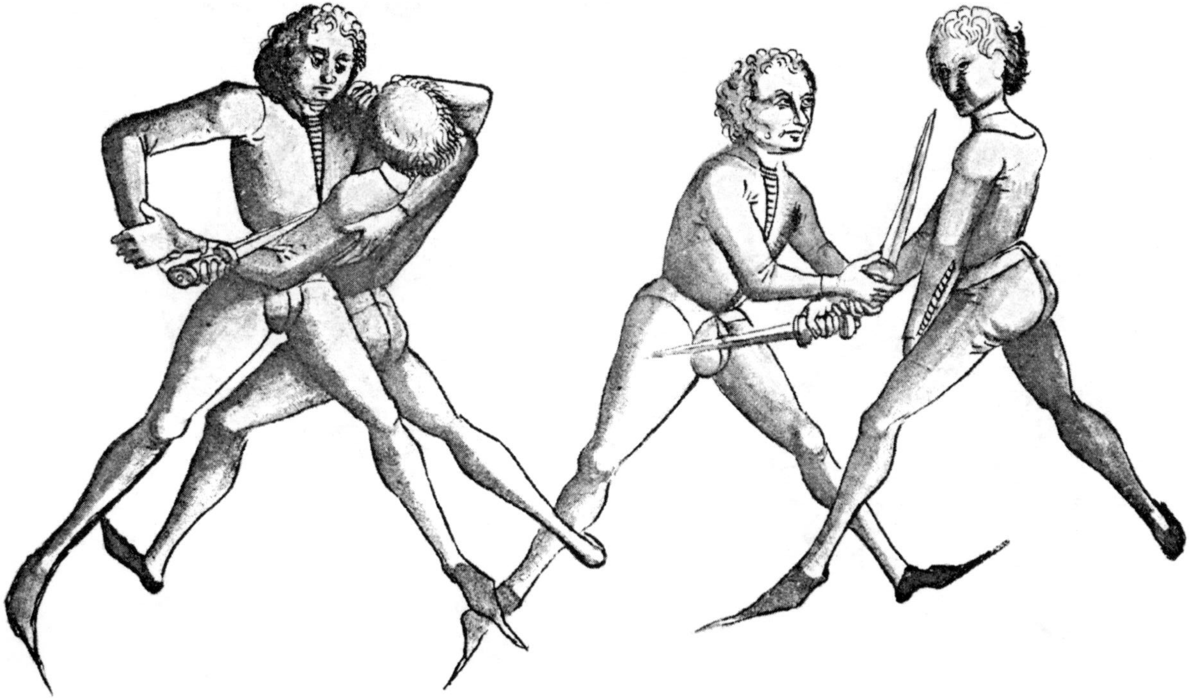

The fighter on the far left counters the stab from below by striking it away with his right hand and grappling his left arm around his opponent's neck and stepping forward to throw him. The fighter second from the right counters the stab from below by trapping it with both hands. He should pivot and break his adversary's arm over his left shoulder.

Plate 181

The fighter on the far left breaks his adversary's arm over his left shoulder, as described above. The fighter on the far right makes a shield against stabs from above and below by gripping his dagger with both hands.

Plate 182

The fighter on the far left makes a shield with his dagger to ward his opponent's cut from above. His opponent counters by twisting his dagger around between his adversary's arms. He now has leverage to throw or disarm his adversary, as we can see in the pair on the right.

Plate 183

The fighter on the far left traps his opponent with the scissors-hold. The fighter second from the right has his opponent in a scissors-hold around the neck. The fighter on the far right will counter by throwing his adversary.

Plate 184

The fighter on the far left blocks his opponent's stab from above with a dagger shield. However, his opponent's attack was a feint, and he changes the attack to a stab below the shield. The fighter on the far right also makes a high dagger shield against his opponent's stab from above. His adversary counters by grappling both his arms and throwing him.

Plate 185

The fighter on the far left counters his opponent's thrust from above by setting aside the thrust with his right arm. On the right we see the counter completed as he grapples his opponent's dagger arm down and gets his own dagger behind his opponent's knee to throw him.

Plate 186

The fighter on the far left catches his opponent's stab with a scissors-hold. The fighter second from the right stands on guard. His opponent on the far right hides his dagger behind his back to confuse his adversary, and may attack with either hand.

Plate 187

The fighter on the far left counters his opponent's stab from above by setting aside the blow with his left arm and grappling his adversary below the thigh with his right arm to throw him. The pair on the right perform the same manoeuvre. The Master (Talhoffer) has himself overseen this work.

Plate 188

The fighter on the far left counters the stab from above by setting it aside with his left arm and grappling his opponent about the neck with his right arm and choking him to the ground. On the right he finishes his opponent off by stabbing him in the neck.

Plate 189

X. WRESTLING:[42] PLATES 190–221

The pair on the left prepare to wrestle. The fighter second from the right sets aside his opponent's thrust from above with his left arm and stabs him in the chest.

Plate 190

The pair on the left are in a clinch, each with one arm on top and one arm below. The wrestler second from the right has slipped his head through his opponent's arms and lifts him.

Plate 191

The fighter second from the left throws his right arm over his opponent's right elbow and grasps under his right knee and throws him over. The fighter second from the right is in a bad position and his opponent is going to throw him over his thigh.

Plate 192

The wrestler on the far left traps his opponent's arm to break it. The wrestler on the far right carries his opponent's arm over his shoulder to break it.

Plate 193

The wrestler on the far left gets his opponent in a hold and throws him over his thigh. The wrestler second from the right steps behind his opponent, grips him by the waist and throws him backward over his thigh.

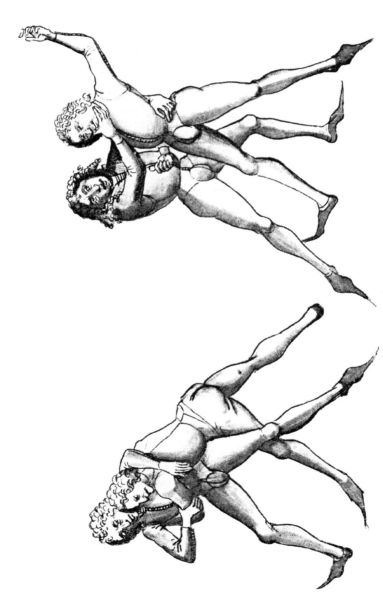

Plate 194

Again, the clinch with each wrestler having one arm on top and one arm below. The wrestler second from the right quickly slips from beneath his opponent's arm, grasps him by the head, and swings him away from himself.

Plate 195

In this hold, the wrestler on the far left means to pass through below his opponent's arm. On the right, the wrestler has passed through and throws his adversary over his back.

Plate 196

The wrestler on the far left counters his adversary's attempt to pass through by gripping him about the neck and choking him. The wrestler second from the right counters the pass through by quickly pivoting and grappling his adversary about the neck and between the legs.

Plate 197

The wrestler second from the left hooks his opponent's leg to throw him. On the right, the hook is countered with a blow with the arm.

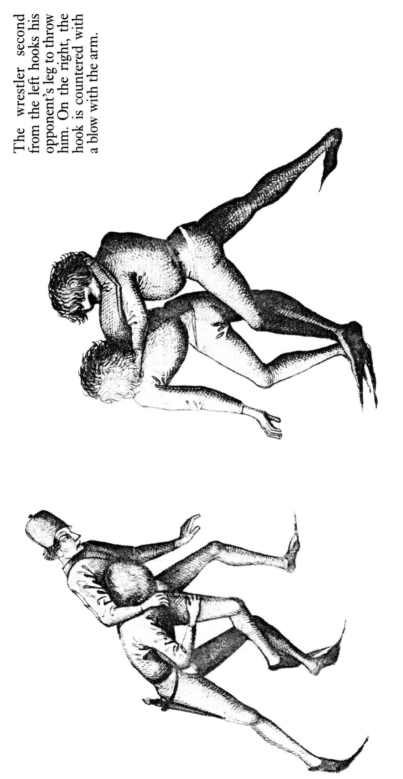

Plate 198

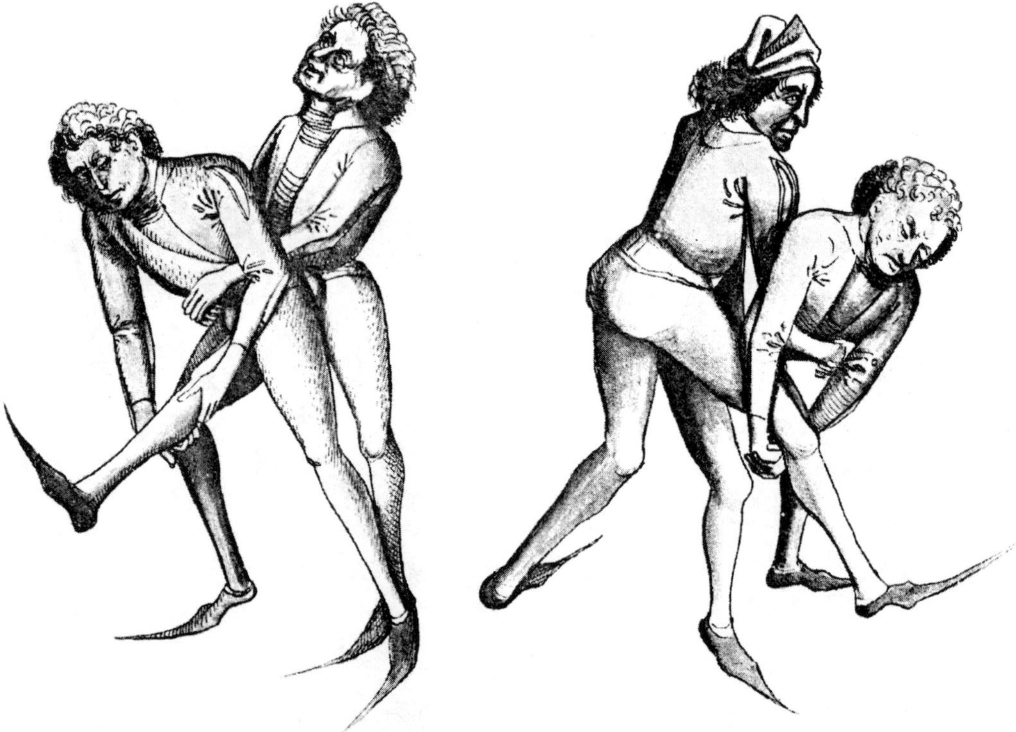

Plate 199

The wrestler on the far left is caught in a hold from behind. He counters by gripping his opponent's leg and drawing it through the fork of his own legs to throw him. The wrestler on the far right counters the hold from behind by stepping backward with his foot between his adversary's legs to grasp his opponent's thigh and throw him.

The pair on the left are in a hoist from behind. To counter it, grasp your opponent by the hair and pull him over your shoulder. The pair on the right are in a lock. If you mean to be free from it, break your opponent's fingers or crouch and throw him over the back.

Plate 200

On the left, when your opponent gets you in a hold to hoist you with both of his arms under yours, grasp his face with both hands and shove him away until he releases you. The wrestler second from the right allows himself to be gripped around the neck and then throws his opponent.

Plate 201

On the left, the wrestler throws his opponent by hooking his leg with his own. On the right, the throw is completed.

Plate 202

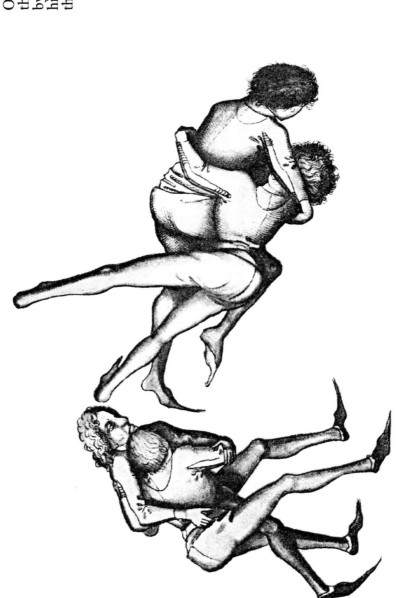

The wrestler on the far left has his opponent in a lock and throws him over his hip. The wrestler second from the right is in the same lock and counters by gripping his opponent below the thigh to throw him.

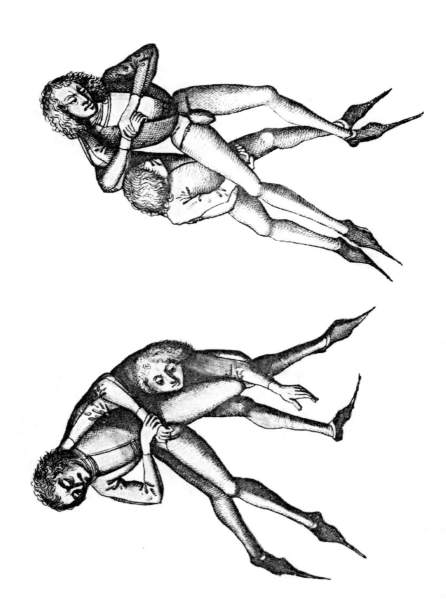

Plate 203

The wrestler on the far left steps behind his opponent to throw him. On the right, the wrestlers are in a clinch and the wrestler second from the right is going to sweep his opponent's foot from beneath him.

Plate 204

The wrestler second from the left hoists his opponent up to spin him around. This is called 'dizzy-wrestling'. The wrestler second from the right grasps his opponent by the throat with both hands to shake him.

Plate 205

On the left we see that it is difficult to hoist an opponent when he is horizontal. On the right is an arm lock, as with the dagger.

Plate 206

This plate shows 'knave wrestling' (see plate 86). The wrestler on the right counters by trapping his opponent with his knee in his groin.

Plate 207

The wrestler on the far left traps his opponent's arm to throw him. The wrestler second from the right counters by getting on the other side of his opponent and throwing him backward over his thigh.

Plate 208

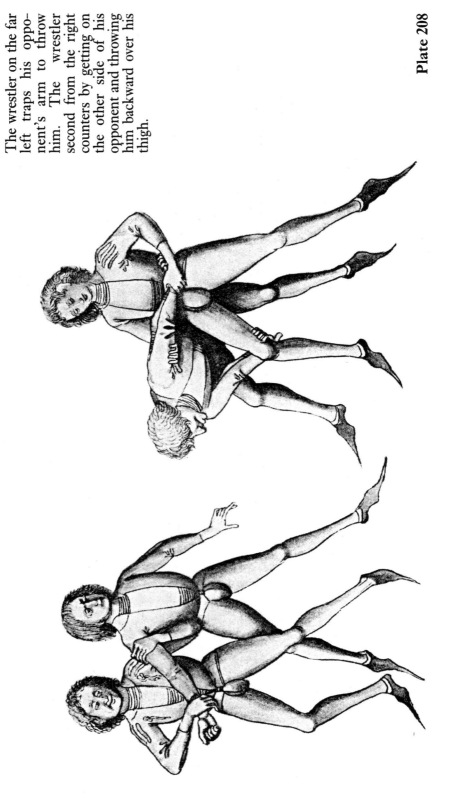

The wrestler on the far left tried to pass through, but his opponent counters by grasping him around the waist and pressing him down. The wrestler on the far right counters a throat hold by putting his opponent in an arm lock.

Plate 209

The wrestler on the far left kicks his opponent in the thigh. The wrestler on the far right grapples his opponent over the shoulder and between the legs to hoist and throw him.

Plate 210

The wrestler second from the left seizes his opponent by the collar and trips him with his right foot. On the right, the throw is completed.

Plate 211

The wrestler second from the left hoists his opponent's arm to trap it between his opponent's legs. On the right, the attack is completed.

Plate 212

The wrestler on the far left traps his opponent's arm. On the right, he completes the attack by grappling his opponent around the throat to throw him backward over his hip.

Plate 213

The wrestler on the far left counters a hold from behind by stepping backward between his adversary's legs and throwing him over his hip. The wrestler second from the right holds both his adversary's arms behind his back.

Plate 214

The wrestler on the far left counters a throat hold by grasping his opponent on the elbow, stepping toward him, and throwing him over his thigh. The wrestler second from the right steps behind his adversary, placing his left arm upon his throat, and throwing him backward over his thigh.

Plate 215

The pair on the left are in a leg hook. On the right, to counter the leg hook, grasp your opponent over the shoulder and throw him over your hip.

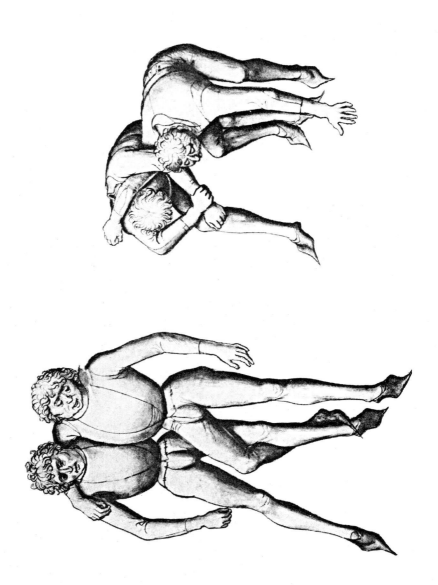

Plate 216

This plate illustrates two ways to counter the leg hook or the throw over the hip.

Plate 217

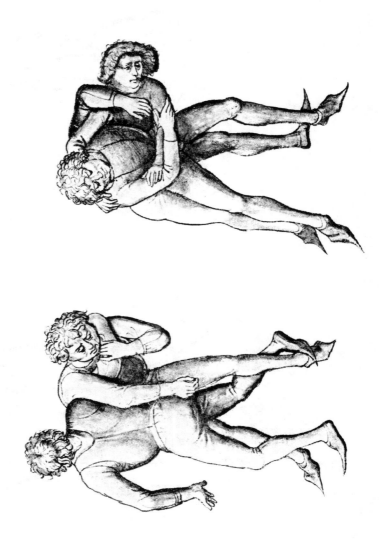

The wrestler on the left completes his counter against the leg hook. The wrestler on the right pivots to counter the leg hook and throws his opponent backward over the hip.

Plate 218

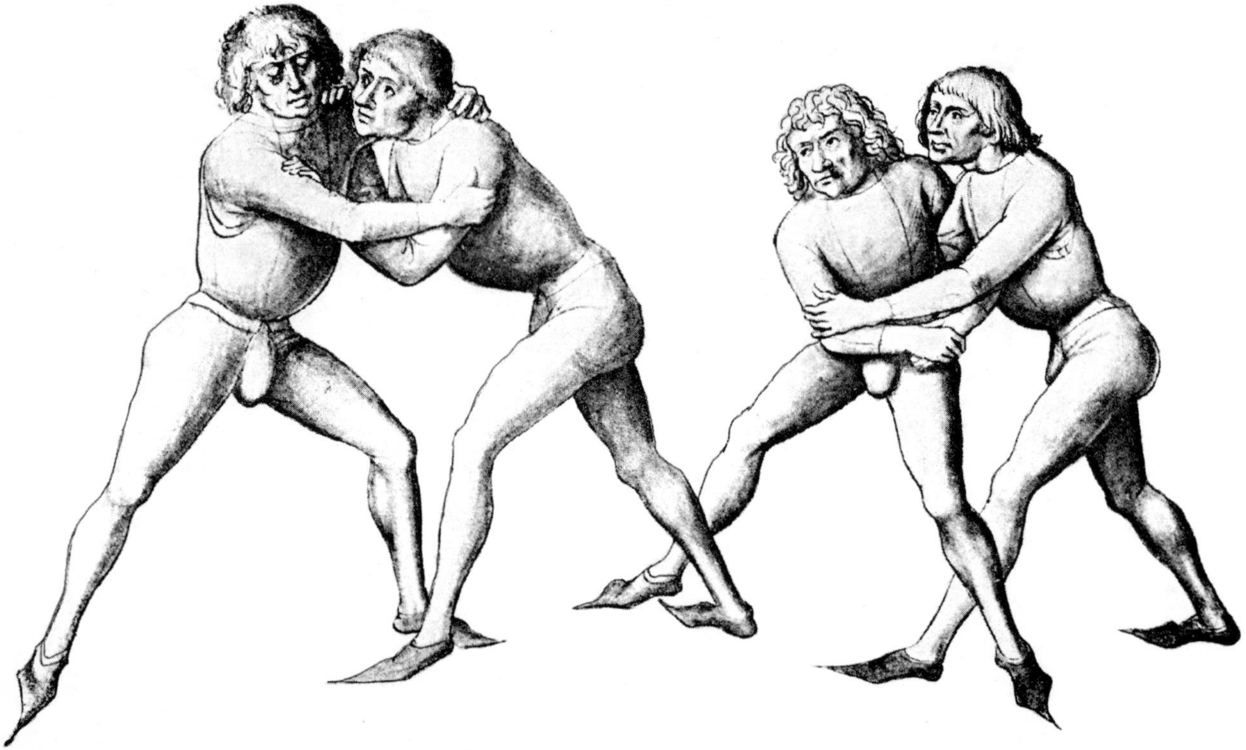

The wrestler on the far left breaks free of a throat grip. On the right he locks his opponent's arm behind him and throws him over his thigh.

Plate 219

The wrestler on the far left grapples his opponent and throws him over his hip. The wrestlers on the right come to grips at the same time, but the wrestler on the far right reaches over his opponent's right arm with his elbow and traps him behind his thigh to throw him.

Plate 220

The throw mentioned above is completed. To counter the leg hook, trap your opponent in the hollow of the knee with your knee (this technique is not illustrated).

Plate 221

XI. MESSER:[43] PLATES 223–30

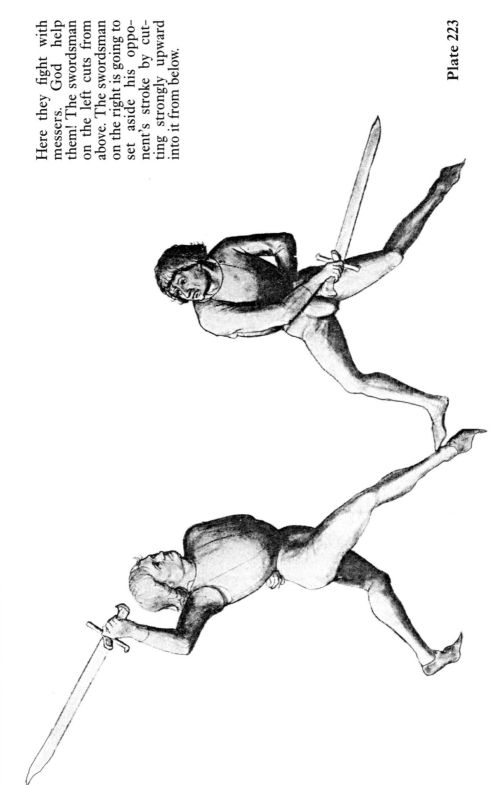

Here they fight with messers. God help them! The swordsman on the left cuts from above. The swordsman on the right is going to set aside his opponent's stroke by cutting strongly upward into it from below.

Plate 223

The swordsman on the left completes his cut. The swordsman on the right sets aside the cut and steps in to grapple his opponent.

Plate 224

The swordsman on the right envelops and locks his opponent's sword arm and cuts him across the head, completing the attack and counter-attack.

Plate 225

The swordsman on the left cuts from above. The swordsman on the right sets the cut aside with a turned-around hand and will step forward and wrench his blade around to the other side.[4]

Plate 226

The swordsman on the right has stepped forward and wrenched his blade around his opponent's blade and pushes his adversary away by the elbow.

Plate 227

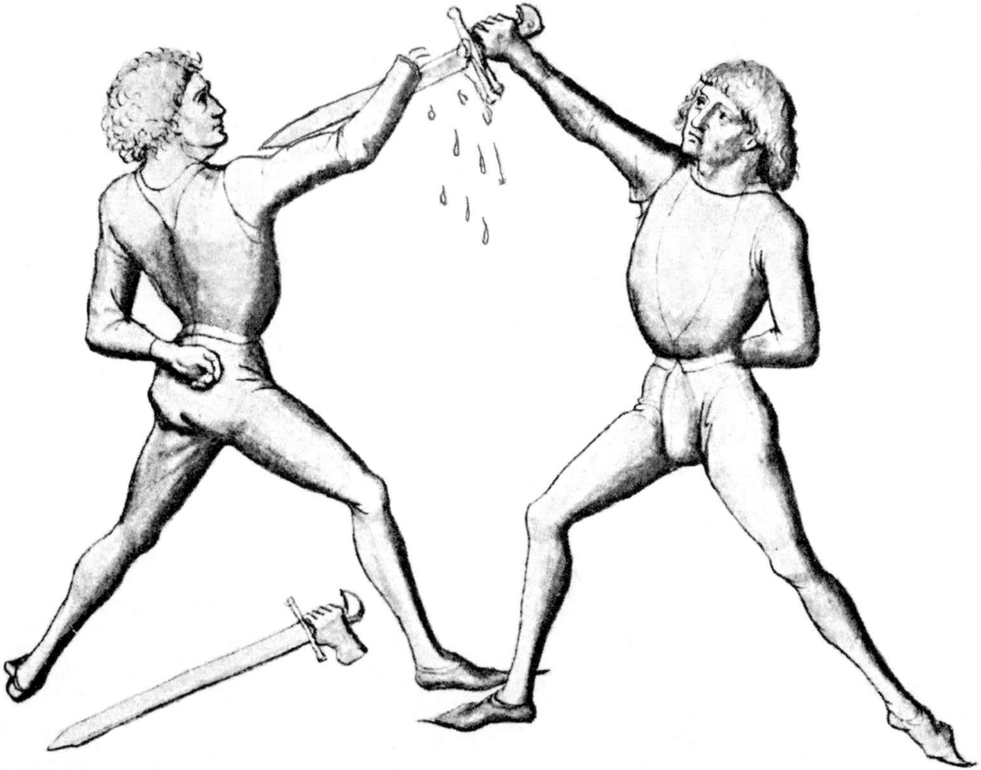

The swordsman on the left charges in with a cut of wrath aimed at his opponent's head.[45] The swordsman on the right sets the blow aside by cutting into it strongly from below, and in doing so, hews off his adversary's hand.

Plate 228

The swordsman on the right steps in and strikes his opponent to death.

Plate 229

The swordsman on the right cuts from above. The swordsman on the left sets aside the cut and grapples his opponent's sword arm, thrusting him in the guts with his messer.

Plate 230

XII. SWORD AND BUCKLER:[46] PLATES 231–39

The swordsmen are in two open stances with the sword and buckler.

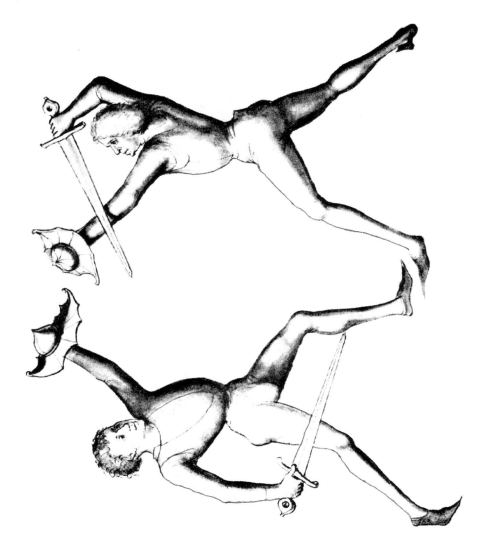

Plate 231

The swordsman on the right cuts from above. The swordsman on the left sets aside the cut with the sword and buckler together. His next move should be to grapple his opponent.

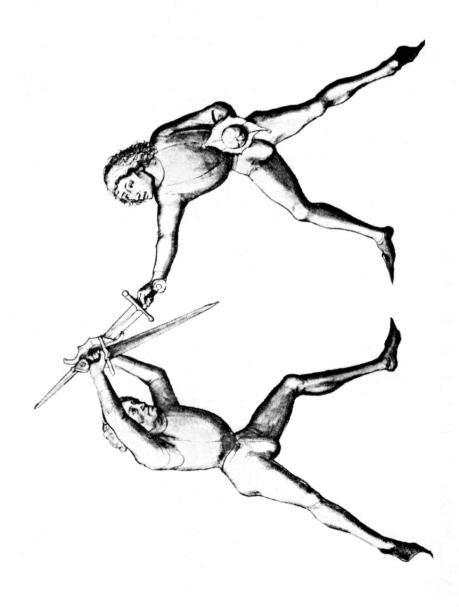

Plate 232

The swordsman on the left cuts from above, so the swordsman on the right sets the cut aside and grapples and locks his sword arm with his buckler arm and cuts his opponent across the head.

Plate 233

The swordsman on the left sets aside his opponent's cut from above, shoves him away, and is going to wrench his blade around for a counter-attack.

Plate 234

The swordsman on the left shoves his opponent away with his buckler on his elbow and finishes the counter-attack by thrusting across himself into his adversary's back.

Plate 235

The swordsman on the left makes another cut from above. The swordsman on the right sets aside the cut with both sword and buckler, and rushes into his opponent.

Plate 236

The swordsman on the right has rushed in and grappled and locked his opponent's sword arm, and thrust into him.

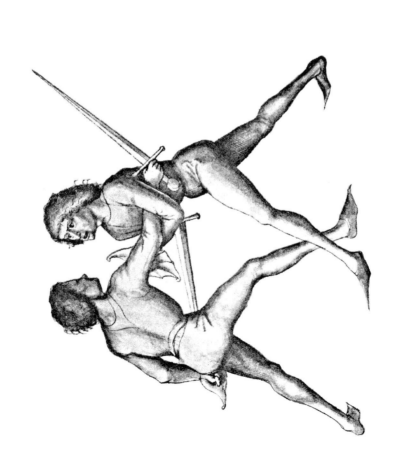

Plate 237

The swordsman on the right thrusts at his opponent. The swordsman on the left stands ready to receive a thrust.[47]

Plate 238

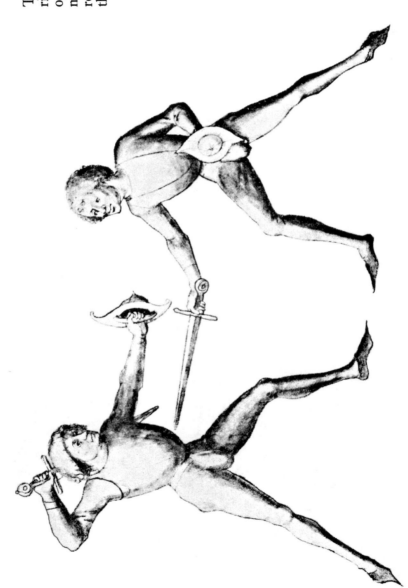

As the swordsman on the right thrusts, the swordsman on the left cuts him in the fore-arm. The cut from above is also good against the thrust.

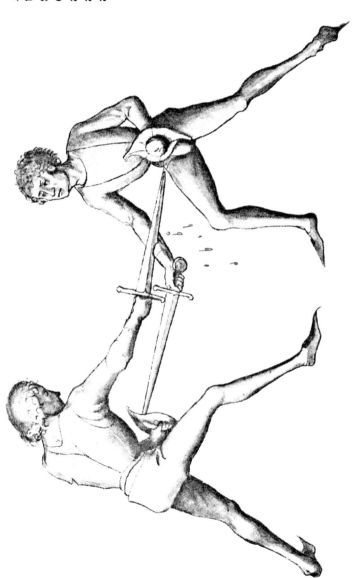

Plate 239

XIII. ONE AGAINST TWO: PLATES 240–1

The swordsman in the centre is in the proper stance to fight two opponents at the same time. Both attackers cut from above. The combatant on the left cuts first and the swordsman in the centre sets aside his blow with a turned-around hand and will pivot to cut the attacker behind him. The swordsman in the centre keeps his dagger and buckler in his left hand to protect his back.

Plate 240

The swordsman in the centre pivots and cuts his adversary on the right across the head. He must pivot again and hew down the remaining attacker.

Plate 241

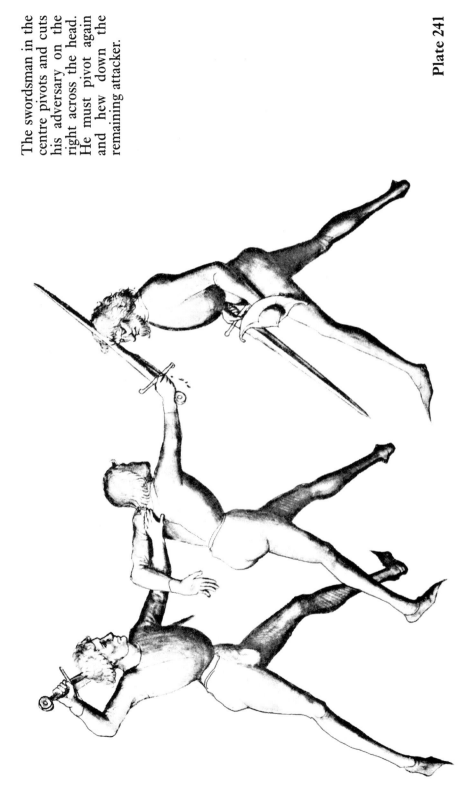

XIV. FIGHT BETWEEN A MAN AND A WOMAN:[48] PLATES 242–50

These are the opening positions for the judicial duel between a man and a woman. The man must stand in a pit up to his waist, armed with a wooden mace. The woman stands above him on the ground with a four- or five-pound stone tied in her veil.

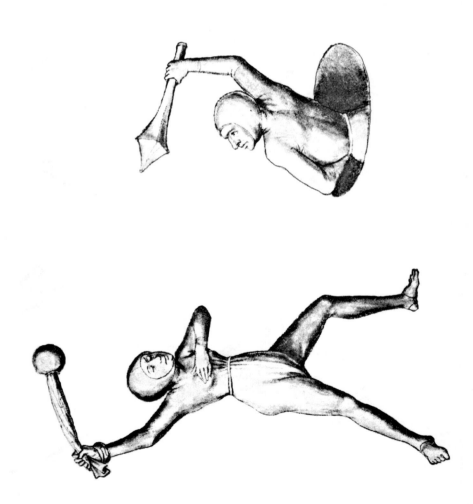

Plate 242

The woman swings
her stone at the man.
He lets the veil wrap
around his arm to pull
her down to himself.

Plate 243

The man pulls the woman toward the pit and throws himself on top of her to strangle her.

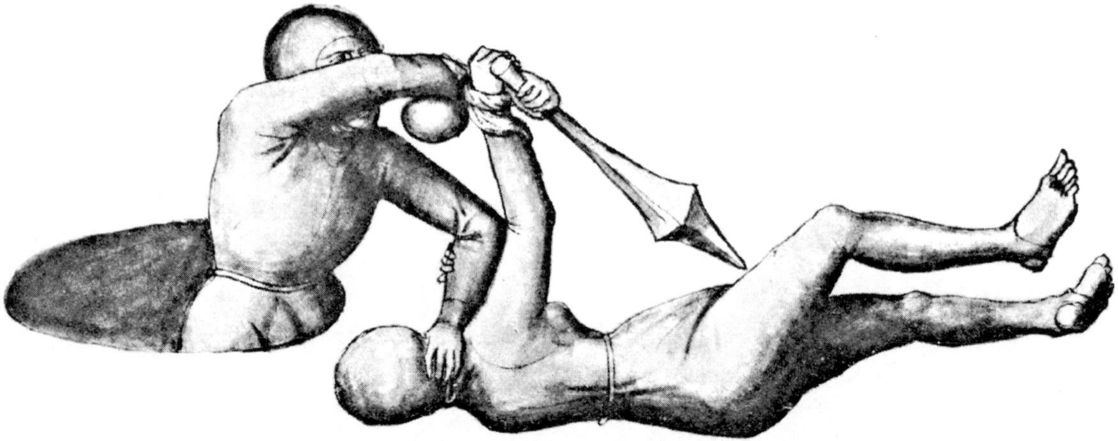

Plate 244

The woman breaks free of the man's hold and gets her arm around his neck to strangle him.

Plate 245

The woman has grasped the man's head from behind to pull him out of the pit onto his back and strangle him.

Plate 246

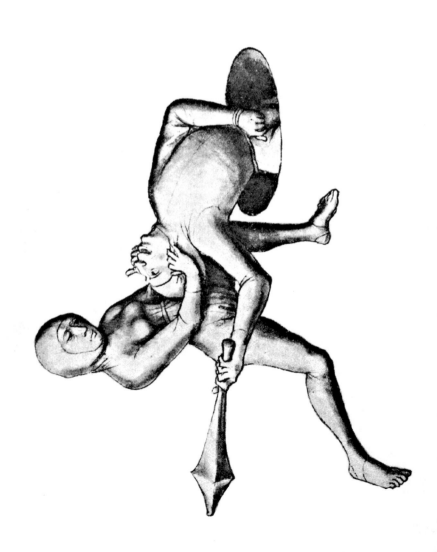

The man pulls the woman to him and throws her into the pit.

Plate 247

The woman moves in to strike the man with her stone. But she steps in too close and the man grasps her by the leg to throw her to the ground.

Plate 248

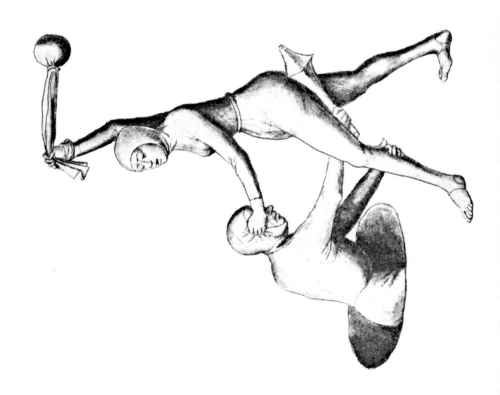

The woman winds her veil around the man's throat to strangle him, but the man strikes her in the chest with his mace.

Plate 249

The woman has the man locked in a hold by the neck and the groin and pulls him out of the pit.

Plate 250

XV. SWORD FIGHT ON HORSEBACK:[49] PLATES 251–60

The horseman on the right charges in to make a cut of wrath (see note 45). The horseman on the left will counter his opponent's cut with a thrust.

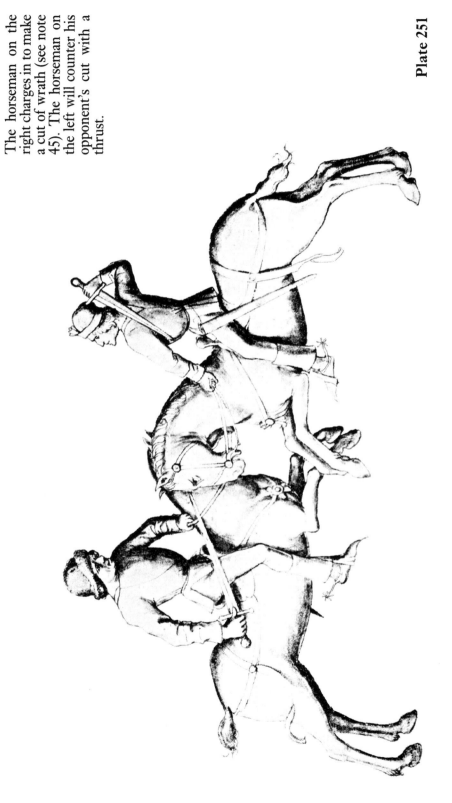

Plate 251

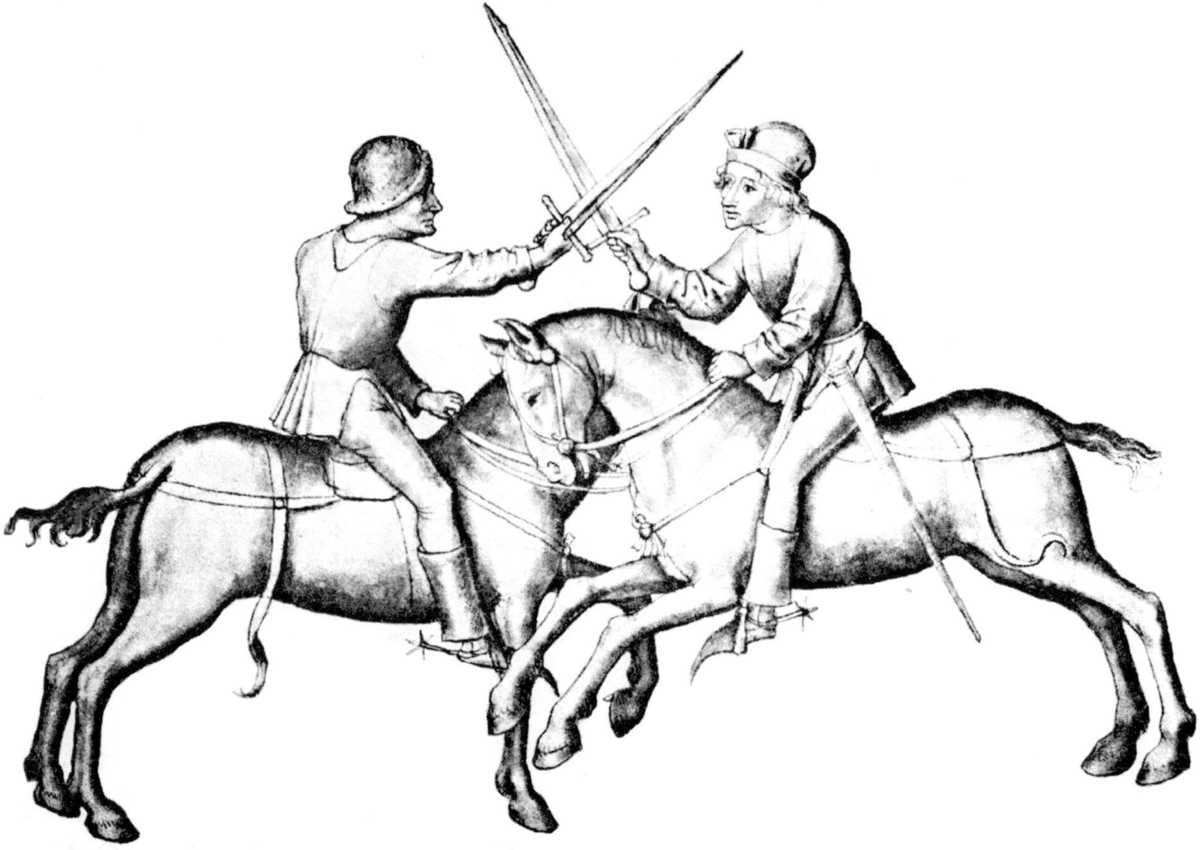

The horseman on the right cuts from above. The horseman on the left sets aside the cut with a cut from below with a turned-around hand.

Plate 252

The horseman on the right completes the sequence described above by wrenching his sword around to cut his opponent on the leg.

Plate 253

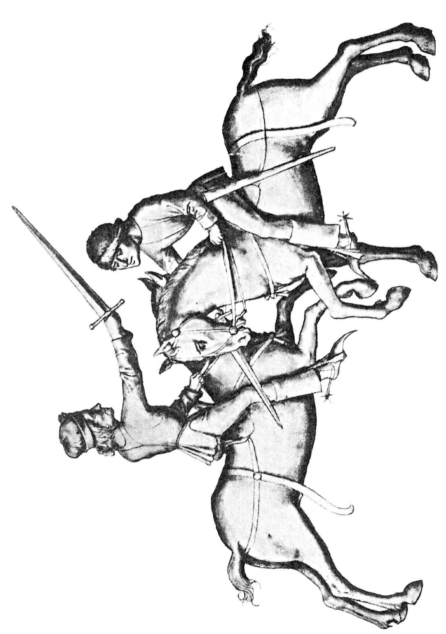

The horseman on the right cuts from above. Charging in, the swordsman on the left catches his opponent's cut and twists his sword into his face.

Plate 254

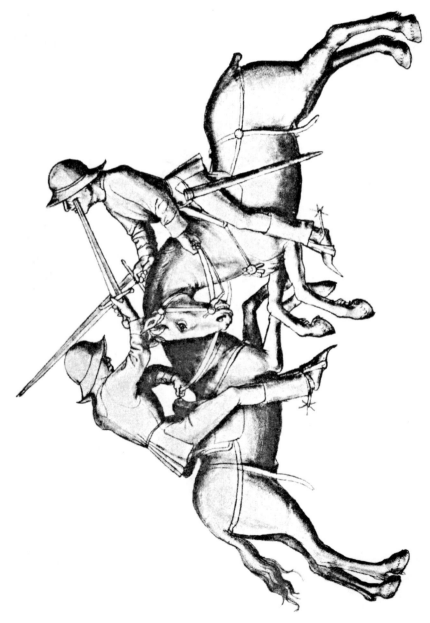

The horseman on the left sets aside his opponent's cut, traps his sword, and wrenches it away from him.

Plate 255

The horseman on the right captures his opponent's sword under his arm.

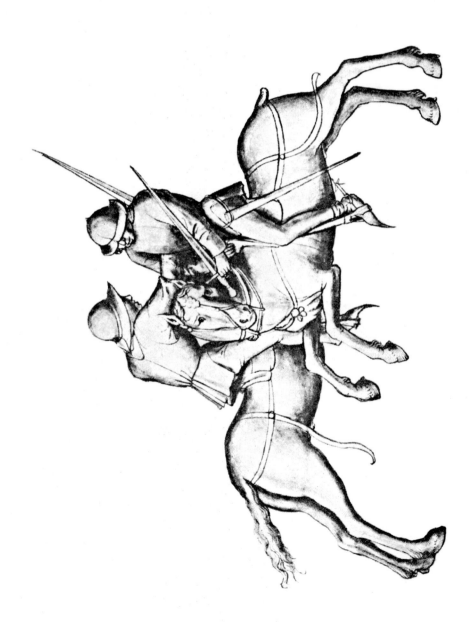

Plate 256

The horseman on the left captures his opponent's sword from behind.

Plate 257

The horseman on the left cuts from above. The horseman on the right counters by setting aside the blow to his right and trapping his opponent about the neck with his sword.

Plate 258

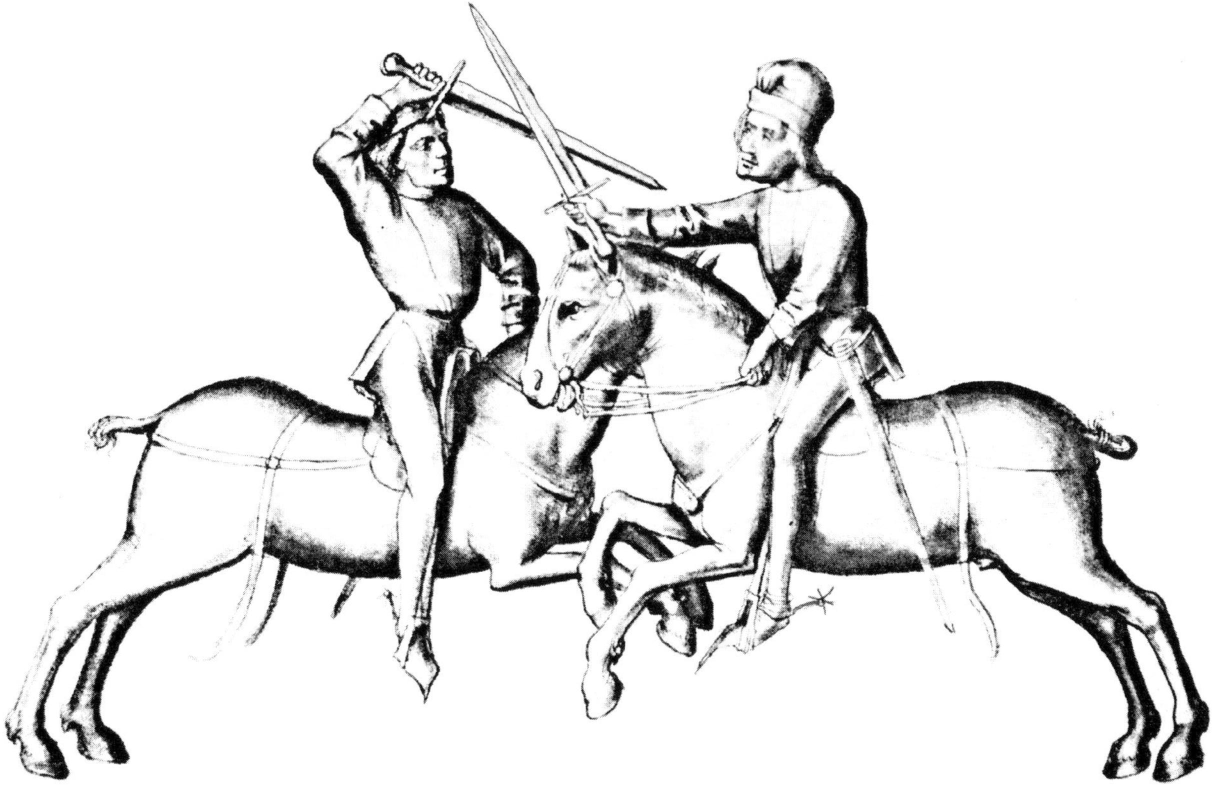

The horseman on the right cuts from above. The horseman on the left sets aside the cut with a hanging guard and will fall upon his opponent.[50]

Plate 259

The horseman on the left falls upon his oppo-nent, completing the attack described above.

Plate 260

XVI. HAND-TO-HAND FIGHT ON HORSEBACK: PLATES 261–4

The horseman on the right wrestles his opponent and gets him in a hold under his arm.

Plate 261

The horseman on the left counters the hold described above and grapples his opponent about the neck.

Plate 262

The horseman on the right has taken hold of the reins of his opponent's horse and charges forward to throw both horse and man.

Plate 263

The horsemen have each other in an arm-lock.

Plate 264

XVII. FIGHT ON HORSEBACK WITH LANCE AND SWORD: PLATES 265–6

The horseman on the right defends himself against the lance by setting it aside with his sword.

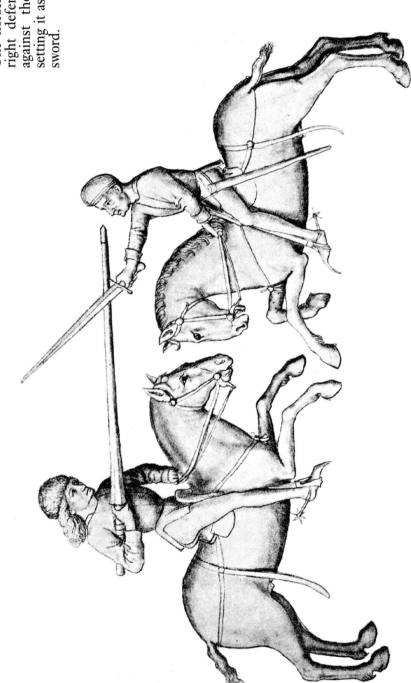

Plate 265

The horseman on the right now has control of his opponent's lance and may thrust at him with his sword.

Plate 266

XVIII. FIGHT ON HORSEBACK AGAINST THE CROSSBOW: PLATES 267–70

This shows how one should behave while in flight while armed with the crossbow.

Plate 267

The lancer on the left charges. The crossbowman discharges his bolt, then sets aside his opponent's lance with his crossbow and prepares to grapple his adversary about the neck.

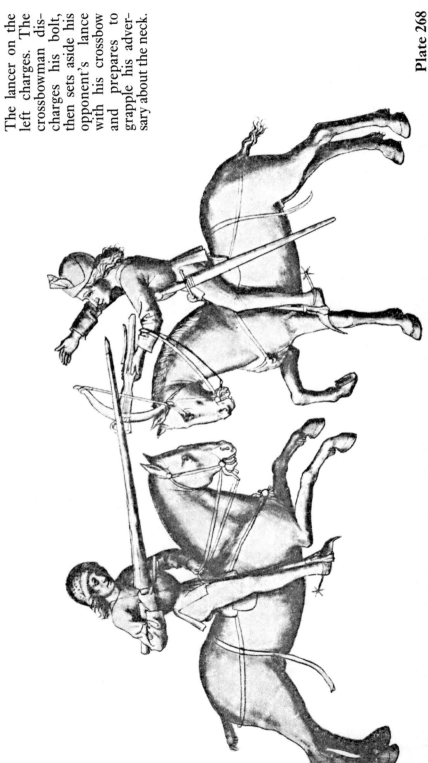

Plate 268

The crossbowman prepares to receive his opponent's attack. The lancer is in the correct position to attack the crossbowman (he uses his lance to cover his body and circles behind the crossbowman to attack him from the rear).

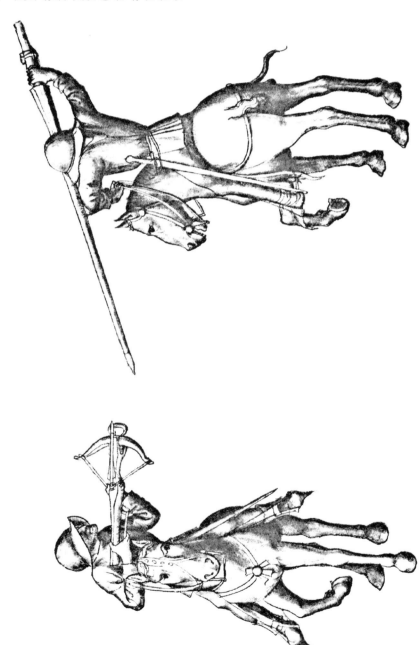

Plate 269

The attack described in plate 268 is completed. The crossbowman grapples the lancer about the neck and disarms him.

– This book was written by Hans Talhoffer, who posed for this portrait.

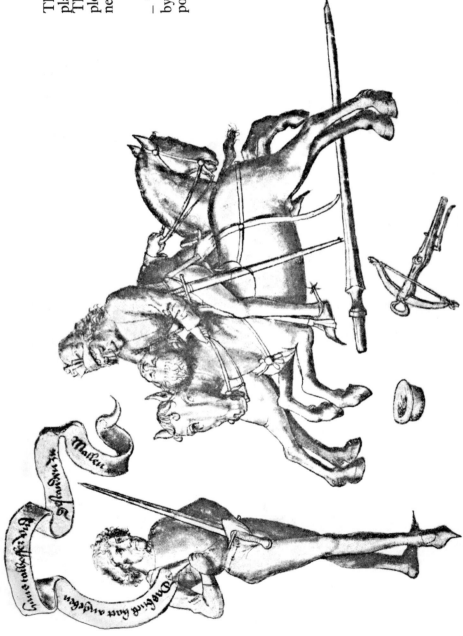

Plate 270

NOTES TO PLATE CAPTIONS

1. The long sword, bastard sword, or hand-and-a-half sword is the quintessential medieval German weapon. This weapon is generally four to five feet long, double-edged and sharply tapered. Talhoffer's long sword has a simple cross guard. The grip is long enough to accommodate both hands, though it may be managed with only one. Contrary to popular notions of this weapon, the medieval long sword is surprisingly light, weighing an average of only three pounds, and capable of blindingly fast attacks. The techniques for its use may be applied to every other edged or pole weapon in the medieval warrior's arsenal.

2. The plunging cut is made from above with the false or back edge of the sword.

3. In medieval swordsmanship every attack is met with an immediate counter-attack that is both offensive and defensive at the same time.

4. The shifting cut is one in which the attack changes direction as it is being made, passing around the opposing blade.

5. The thrust of wrath is a powerful downward diagonal thrust from the right (see note 45).

6. The crosswise thrust is made by pivoting the sword so that the right wrist crosses above the left wrist. In general, actions that result in the crossing of the arms or wrists are weaker than uncrossed actions. See also plate 31.

7. This is an example of the medieval custom of using mnemonic devices for naming actions of the sword. The cut from the roof moves vertically downward.

8. The body is divided into four openings or targets: upper and lower at the horizontal line of the ribcage, right and left at the vertical axis of the body.

9. A cut must arrive with a step of the foot from the same side as the cut originates. This allows the weight of the body and the torque of the hips to set the cut. In plate 9, the swordsman on the right is cutting from left to right, timing the cut to land with a step forward with his left foot. This has the additional defensive advantage of interposing his blade between himself and the enemy's steel. I am indebted to Norbert Krines of Bamberg, Germany, for his insight into this caption. See also Introduction note 9.

10. The bind is a crossing of weapons with opposition or pressure.

11. The iron gate (*eisen port, porto di ferro*) is a basic defensive guard with the long sword, protecting the legs and lower body.

12. The crooked cut is a downward cut made with the false or back edge of the blade, causing the swordsman's wrists to twist.

13. This plate illustrates the brutal reality of long sword fighting: two adversaries locked closely together in a life-and-death embrace from which only one may emerge alive.

14. The hanging guard (*ochs*, or 'ox') is made with the hands held high and close to the side of the head and the blade covering the body diagonally downward and directed toward the opponent. See plates 6, 13, 14, and 259 for other examples.

15. The half-sword was originally used against an armoured opponent. The sword is gripped on the blade with the left hand and wielded like a short spear. This technique is effective for close work, punching through chinks in armour (*ie* at the face, groin, armpits, joints etc) and attacks on the opponent's sword. See also note 21.

16. The coat of arms at the side of this plate is Swabian, bearing the date 1467. 'The arms are quartered: the first and fourth fields are gold with three black antlers upon each, representing the County of Württemberg; the second and third fields are red with two golden barbs upon each, representing the County of Mümpelgard. The crest surmounting the arms consists of a red closed helm and a gold-streaked trumpet to which is appended a black cord interwoven with gold. From out of the mouthpiece of the horn are three ostrich feathers: blue, white and red. The helmet drape is red and gold.' – Gustav Hergsell, *Talhoffers Fechtbuch aus dem Jahre 1467*.

17. The murder-stroke is a forceful blow struck by reversing the sword and gripping it by the blade with both hands in order to use the hilt as a hammer to pound through the opposing guard. Similar to the thunderclap stroke.

18. The squinting guard is one in which the sword is held close to the head with the blade parallel to the ground and pointing at the opponent, causing the swordsman to 'squint' down the length of his blade.

19. Another guard with a mnemonic name. In the *brentschirn* or the bind with the shortened sword, the blade is gripped by the left hand and carried with the point angled upward.

20. False in this case refers to a feint or fake attack designed to provoke a response from the opponent that can be exploited.

21. The translator has witnessed a demonstration of a sharp blade being held with a bare hand. As long as the blade is gripped firmly and not allowed to draw through the hand, the sword may be held securely in this manner, withstanding efforts to pull it away.

22. In this action the sword is shifted to the left hand so that the opponent's blade may be seized with the right hand.

23. *Versetzen*, to set aside, is another basic technique of medieval swordplay. Rather than meeting the oncoming blow with a solid block, it is set aside, displaced, or parried (to use the modern term) with an action that is both defensive and offensive at the same time.

24. This is a judicial combat or 'trial by battel' between noblemen in full armour using swords and spears. The 'lists' are the barriers within which the combat occurs.

25. The ceremonial display of the coffins underscores the lethal nature of trial by combat.

26. This is the fundamental principle of German swordplay: every attack is met with an immediate counter-attack which also serves as a defence.

27. The pole-axe takes many forms, but usually consists of an axe blade or hammer head and several sharp spikes affixed to a long pole partially sheathed in iron. Talhoffer's weapon is a 'Lucerne hammer', having a v-shaped notch in the forward hammer-like blade.

28. One interpretation of this manoeuvre is that the combatant on the left binds his opponent with the shaft of his weapon, disengages and swings the blade of his pole-axe into his adversary's head.

29. This is another form of ritual or judicial combat. Following the law of the Franks, the combatants are barefoot and stitched into tight-fitting cowled leather suits, upon the front and back of which appears the cross. They are armed with a large wooden club or mace and a special duelling shield. The shield is an oblong approximately six-and-a-half feet tall, slightly concave (see plate 149), with a rectangular coffered boss along the longitudinal axis allowing room for the hand to grip a central pole which is sharply spiked at both ends. The shield is made of wood, possibly covered with cloth or leather, and also bears the image of the cross.

30. A similar combat to the one before, except that the mace has been replaced with the long sword, according to the Swabian law. There is no Plate 127.

31. Possibly Schwabische Hall, a Swabian town which is the site of the largest fortified medieval church in Germany.

32. Note that the combatant on the left has his index finger hooked over the cross guard of his sword for better control.

33. A crosswise cut is a diagonal downward cut that moves across the body from right to left, forcing the swordsman's arms to cross.

34. This section illustrates techniques for fighting with the shield alone.

35. The combatant on the left is using a throated hooking shield (see note 38).

36. The combatants hold their shields with their arms reversed from the normal stance, allowing them to spin their shields.

37. The concept of weak versus strong (*schweche und starke*) is another basic principle of the German art of fighting. A sword is strong toward the hilt and weak toward the point. A shield or pole-arm is strong between the hands and weak outside the hands. Strong and weak also may refer to the pressure exerted by the weapons in a bind. A combatant may use the strong force of his weapon to create an opening against the weak force of his opponent's weapon. A combatant may also exploit the strong force of his opponent's weapon against the weak force of his own weapon to disengage suddenly and gain an advantage over his adversary. It is a deadly game of leverage, timing and judgement.

38. Perhaps the most bizarre weapon in Talhoffer's arsenal, the throated hooking shield is a cello-shaped affair with four protruding hooks for catching, pulling and stabbing one's opponent. Like the duelling shield, it has a long sharply spiked pole for a hand-hold and a rectangular coffered boss. The translator has seen these shields demonstrated and can assure the reader that they are formidably effective.

39. Talhoffer shows a 'rondel' dagger, with two flanges at either end of the grip and an extremely long triangular blade which may be held with the off-hand for blocks and locks.

40. The shield is a block made by holding the dagger with one hand on the grip and one hand on the blade, as with the half-sword. See also note 15.

41. The scissors-hold is a dagger lock in which the attacker's dagger hand is captured by the defender blocking the stab with his dagger arm, hooking his own dagger around the back of the attacker's wrist or forearm and closing the lock by grasping his own dagger blade with his unarmed hand.

42. More than a third of all the plates illustrating armed combat include some kind of grappling, demonstrating how important wrestling is to the German art of fighting. Talhoffer borrows his wrestling techniques from Ott, an earlier wrestling master to the Habsburg Dukes of Austria.

43. The German messer or 'long knife' is a single-edged, single-handed sword with a simple cross guard. The blade is slightly curved and the last few inches of the clipped back or false edge are sharp. It resembles the ancient saxe, falchion, Italian storta, dusak (a wooden training weapon of Bohemian origin), or Polish sabre, and was carried as an everyday side-arm by commoners in medieval Germany. The artist Albrecht Dürer devotes a large section of his *Fechtbuch* to the messer (see bibliography). There is no Plate 222.

44. In this manoeuvre, the swordsman cuts into his opponent's attack from below with his palm up, and then quickly snaps his messer around to the other side as the initial attack passes harmlessly by. The defender is now behind his adversary and has him at his mercy.

45. The cut of wrath is a powerful downward diagonal cut from the right. In preparation for the cut, the sword point is dropped behind the back.

46. This section illustrates the use of the single-handed sword and the buckler, a small shield with a round central boss for the hand. True to form, Talhoffer's bucklers have protruding hooks at top and bottom, which may be used to catch and deflect the opponent's blade.

47. There are two things of note in the illustration of the swordsman on the left. One is that the buckler must be carried well forward from the body to encounter a thrust. The other is that the position of the sword is that from which the cut of wrath is delivered.

48. Truly a bizarre judicial duel. Both opponents are in the tight-fitting leather garments of the trial by combat. The odds are evened by placing the man in a pit up to his waist and arming him with the wooden mace we saw in use with the duelling shields. The woman is armed with a 'rock in a sock', a three-pound stone knotted in her veil, and may move freely about the man on the ground above him. If she succeeds in pulling him out of the pit, his life is forfeit. Likewise, if he manages to pull her down into the pit, she faces instant execution.

49. What follows is a series of techniques for combat on horseback with a variety of weapons and hand-to-hand.

50. See note 14.

APPENDIX

These captions, in the original Swabian, accompany the plates in the
manuscript of Talhoffer's *Fechtbuch* of 1467.

I.   Langes Schwert

1.   Oberhow. – Underhow.
2.   Sturtzhow. – Wechsselhow.
3.   Zorn ortt Im dröw. – Aber oberhout.
4.   Das lang Zorn ortt. – Darfür ist das geschrenckt ortt.
5.   Der fry how von Tach. – Darus das Halsfahen mach.
6.   Am underen blosz. – ouch am underen blosz.
7.   Ain schwert niemen.
8.   Ain zu legen oder eekomen.
9.   Linck gen rechten das must Starck vechten.
10.   Ain fryes ortt. – Das gayszlen.
11.   Usz dem anbinden hinwegstoszen hinter dem Elbogen vassen.
12.   Mit dem fryen ortt Inlouffen und Tretten in den buch.
13.   Zwey ober ortt.
14.   Die zwo underen blosz.
15.   Das wegbinden oder Hinder binden.
16.   Das gryffen über die Iszny Portt. – Die yszni Port.
17.   Den Oberhaw erliegen und In die arm slahen.
18.   Der das geschrenckt ortt macht. – Der hout von tach.
19.   Krum uff behend – das ort wider wend.
20.   Hie ist die krum volbracht.
21.   Der gryfft nach der underen blosz – Der schnit von oben daryn.
22.   Die arbeit Im krieg.
23.   Die geschrenckt schwechin. – Der stat in der Hut.

24.   Ain überfallen.

25.   Stand beid In der Hut.

26.   Ain gewauppet Infallen und swert niemen.

27.   Der staut fry Im ort. – Der hout linck über das ort.

28.   Usz dem oberhow geuallen In das gewauppet ort.

29.   Usz den anbinden ubergryffen und werfen.

30.   Usz den anbinden aber ain vahen mit gewalt.

31.   Usz den anbinden geuallen In die undere ort.

32.   Usz dem anbinden stossen hinweg by den Elbogen.

33.   Der mortschlag.

34.   Der Wurff usz dem ortschlag.

35.   Usz dem fryen How geuallen In das gewauppet ort.

36.   Usz dem schilher geuallen In das gewauppet ort.

37.   Usz dem Tunrschlag Ain werffen. – Usz dem Tunrschlag ain Ryszen.

38.   Nach dem Ryszen der stos In das antlitz.

39.   Das brentschirn. – Oder das anbinden Im kurtzen Schwert.

40.   Usz dem anbinden Im kurtzen schwert.

41.   Usz dem brentschüren ein leinen uff den Elbogen.

42.   Ain Notstand für den Stich oben und unden.

43.   Ain gedreng darus Arbaiten.

44.   Ain hefften In Hentschuch.

45.   Ain Hefften In fus.

46.   Vom anbinden ain Ryszen by der knüw kelen.

47.   Den mordstraich erlogen und schlahen In den schenckel.

48.   Usz dem anbinden ain Halssryszen.

49.   Hie hand sie die swert begriffen.

50.   Ain schwert niemen.

51.   Schwert wechszlen.

52.   Aber ain suchen. – Der wil stossen und Ryszen.

53.   Hie ist der mordstraich versetzt und ryszt In by dem Hals.

54.   Usz dem brentschiren ain ynschlieszenn.

55.   Usz dem swert vassen so würffs baide von dir und vollend.

56.   Vom dem mordstraich das umb kern.

57.   Der Bruch über das umkern.

58.   Usz dem Mordstreich von Im louffen und stoszen und wider schlahen und ryszen.

59.   Usz dem swert begryffen durch schlupffen.

60.   Usz den brentschürn ain schlieszen und werffen.

61.   Der staut für stich und Straich. – Der staut verkert für Stich
       und Streich.

62.   Aber ain schwert niemen.

63.   Der will schlahenn. – Ain Inlouffen.

64.   Usz dem Inlouffen der wurff.

65.   Der wurff Ist volbracht.

66.   Für den stich und rysen In Arm.

67.   Und mit fürtretten und stossen In das antlitz.

II.   Kämpfe in den Schranken mit Spiess und Schwert in voller Rüstung

68.   Hie gat er In den schrancken. – Der tregt Im sin Zug vor.

69.   Hie sitzent sie beid Im schrancken und wartent des anlas und
       hat yeder sin bär hinder Im und sin grieswarten vor Im.

70.   Hie sint sie angelauszen und stat der in der versatzung für den
       schutz. – Der will schiessen mit dem spies.

71.   Der hat geschossen. – Der schusz ist versetzt.

72.   Das versetzen für den schlag. – Der anlouff mit
       dem Mordtschlag.

73.   Usz der versatzung hinweg stossen. – Der haut den
       straich volbracht.

III.   Langes Schwert

74.   Und fürtreten und werffen über den schenckel.

75.   Ain bruch für ain fryen schlag versetz gewaubet und ubergryff
       den man und fall uff den tritten fus.

76.   Stuck und bruch.

77.   Der Zwyuelstich. – Der recht stand in der Nott. – Der wil
       arbeiten. – Der stat In sin vorteil on gewer.

78.   Da Ringen sie umb das swert. – Hie hat der geschlagen und der
       ander versetzt und macht ain end.

IV.   Streitaxt

79.   Das erst anbinden mit der axst.

80.   Usz dem anbinden Hat er In werlousz gemacht.

81.   Der will fry schlahen. – Der will In hinder binden und In
       werlousz machen und sin schlag hinweg helffen.

82.   Hie hat er dem schlag hinweg geholffen, und ist das stuck volbraucht.

83.   Der erlogen straich versetzet und darus geryssen.

84.   Als sie baid geschlagen hand von tach usz dem anbinden so felt
       er Im umb den Hals und ryszt In.

85.   In dem Ryszen dritt der hinach und ergrifft In by dem Hals und
       wurfft In über die Hüfften.

86.   Usz dem anbinden sint sie zu Ringen komen und hat In usz dem
       buben wurff geworffen.

87.   Usz dem fryen schlag und anbinden hat er In übergriffen, und
       will In werffen.

88.   Der hat geslagen. – Hie versetzt der mit dem schafft und will
       arbeiten.

89.   Hie ist er furtreten und das stuck volbracht.

90.   Der hat geschlagen dem nach den füszen. – Der hat den schlag
       versetzt und will wyter arbaiten.

91.   Usz der versatzung schlecht er In an Hals und will Ryszen.

92.   Hie hat der den stich versetzt und schlecht In umb den Hals und
       will ryszen. – Der hat gestochen.

93.   Hie macht der den bruch und ryszen sie sich umb die agst.

94.   Da ist das stuck volbracht und würfft In über den schenckel.

95.   Usz den anbinden felt er Im mit der agst hinder den Elbogen
       und schubt In hinweg.

96.   Da lat er sich gar umb kern und macht den bruch uber das
       vorgenant stuck.

97.   Aber ain anlasz. – Hie will der den nöten mit stichen und
       schlahen.

98.   Hie hat der den stich versetzt und will ryszen.

99.   Ain Hinderbinden.

100.   Der wartet des schlags von Tach. – Der wyl mit macht Schlahen.

101.   Hie hat der den schlag versetzt und stotzt In von Im. – Der hat
       mir Tschwecht In Sterck geben und mich von Im gestossen.

102.   Hie bin ich von mynem vortail komen. – Als er In gestossen hatt
        so schlecht er Im die agst an Halsz und würfft In an den Rucken.
103.   Hie machet er ain enstuck mit Im und Sticht In zu tod.

V.   Schild und Kolben

104.   Hie ist der anfang mit dem schilt und ston in mynem Vortail Gott
        geb uns glük und haill. – Hie ston Ich nach frenckeschem Rechten.
105.   Damit lausz ich mich nit erschrencken. Ich wyl mich mit dem
        schült bedecken. – Hie ston ich Im wurff.
106.   Hie In diser stund hast du mich gar blosz funden. – Hie hatt er
        den schilt geschrenckt und schlecht Im nach Sinem hopt.
107.   Der wyl Im den schilt Inschlahen. – So tritt er für und wyl In zu
        dem hopt schlahen.
108.   Ich bin funden blos. Ich fircht es werd mir ain stosz. – Der hatt
        Im hinder den schilt gebunden.
109.   Hie macht er mir ain endstosz. – Hie hon ich den gestossen.
110.   Mit mynem Tryt hon ich dich entrist, und schlach gar gewyssz. –
        Er hatt mir den schilt umbtretten. So wyl Ich werffen.
111.   Hie wyl der den schilt obnen hinyn stossen. – Hie wil Ich Im
        hinterbinden und umb Sin hertz blos finden.
112.   Hie ist das stuck volbracht wie vor geschriben Stat.
113.   Hie Triben Sie ainannder umb und sucht yeglicher sinem vortail.–
        Der hatt den vortail.
114.   Da hatt er Im den Schilt usz der hend geschlagen usz dem
        anbinden und wyl stossen wa er Im noch blosz finden. – So grifft
        aber der mit dem Arm und würfft den schilt von Im und hilfft
        Im hinweg.
115.   Usz sinem anweg helffen kumpt mir myn stossz herwynder. –
        Hie bin Ich worden blos des wirt mir ain beser Stossz.
116.   Usz dem hinnweghelffen ist das Stuck gantz volbracht.
117.   Die Bindent aber ainannder an.
118.   Usz dem anbinden So hatt er In hinderbunden und Stoszt Im
        mit dem schilt oben durch Sinen schenckel.
119.   Hie statt der In Siner Hutt und wartet des Mans. – So schlecht
        der den Hacken hinder sinen Schilt und zert hindersich.
120.   Der Zert hindersich wie vor geschriben Statt.

121. Usz dem hindersich zeren So stoszt er hinwyder den Schilt In den. Und ist das Stuck volbracht.

122. Hie wurfft er sinen arm uff und übergrifft Im Sin arm und latt den Schilt fallen und Tryt fur und Schlecht Im Sin lincken arm umb Sinen Halsz und wurfft In über die huffen. – Hie kert er den schilt umb und Schlecht geschrenckt dem zu sinem houpt.

123. Hie wirt das Stuck volbracht wie vor geschriben Statt.

124. Der ist ganntz werlosz und wirt geworffen. – Der hatt Sinen schilt swüschen Man und schilt geschlagen und latt den schilt und wyl In werffen.

125. Hie ist der Wurff volbracht und Schlecht In dem kolben.

126. Der hatt Im sinen Straich versetzt mit dem kolben und über gryfft In mit dem Arm und Schlecht In zu tod. – Da Sint sie komen von den schilten und Schlahent ainander mit den kolben. Hie hatt das kolben vechten ain end.

VI.   Schild und Schwert

128. Hie Ston Ich fry Nach Schwebischem rechten. Als man ze Hall vicht. – So ston ich mit schilt und schwert und hon din lang zu fechten begert.

129. Der wyl den Schilt wenden und howen. – So bringt er Sin schwert swüschen die schilt und versucht wie starck er Stand.

130. Der sticht mit geschrencktem Schilt. – Hie statt der blos unversetzt.

131. Wir zwen standen wie die obern wenn das wir uns verkert haben und Statt yeglicher an des anndern Statt.

132. Im verborgen Stand wend Ich min Schilt und schryt für mit dem Stich. – Hie hab ich myn schilt gewendt und bin doch geschent.

133. So zuckt ich mynem Schilt und Tryt usz Sinem treffen damit So tun ich Im sin Stuck Brechen. – Ich hon wöllen geschrenckt Stechen hinder Sinen Schilt.

134. Usz dem anlouffen So Tryt Ich den schilt von dir und hab myn Stich volbracht an dir.

135. Da tun Ich versetzten mit Sterckin wyl ich dir din höw und Stich letzen. – Der hatt den Schilt verkert. Das merck.

136. So lausz ich mynen schilt fallen und how zu der blessin. – Der hatt wöllen zwüschen Schilt Stossen.

137. Hie Ist aber ain end. – So latt aver der sinen schilt och Fallen und ergryfft In by den Elbogen und Stoszt Schwert durch In.

138. So wyll der Schilt und Schwert ynschlahen und hinderbinden ob er In möcht blos finden. – Der statt In siner versatzung.

139. Er hatt mir gezucht das treffen, damit er thut mich Effen. – Hie hon ich Im gezuckt sin Treffen das er hatt gefelt und hon Im nachgerayszt mit dem Stick.

140. So hatt er den Stosz vernomen, und latt In nit dartzu komen. – Der hatt usz dem bochen schwert und schilt zemen genomen ob er Im möcht oben hinyn komen.

141. Da bin Ich zwüschen Schilt und Swert gedrungen, das ich dir zum houpt bin komen. – Als Ich hon gehowen geschrenckt Da Ist mir mysse lungen.

142. Mit schrencken und Schryten wyl er howen. – Hie Merck wie ich das main das ich hon gezuckt und Stich in durch sin bain.

143. Der Statt in der versatzung fry. – In dem stand verborgen wechselt er das Swert In die lincken hand und ersticht In übern schilt.

144. In ainem fryen Stand So bin Ich komen umb myn hand. – Das mag Ich wolgedencken das ich hon gehowen mit Schrencken.

145. Der stant In dem stand dar Inn der kam umb Sin hand. – Aber wyl der uber den schilt winden, ob er in möchte blosz finden.

146. Hie stand wir bayd blos. – Aver der mag den schilt wol hinyn werffen und In von Im stossen.

147. Da hatt er In von Im gestossen vom wurff und vom stosz musz er Sich bucken des how Ich In In Kopff und In Rucken.

148. Der hat wöllen mit schilt und Swert Inbinden und Rysen. – So hatt der hinder sich geruckt und Im usz sinem Inschlahen gezuckt und latt den schilt fallen und Tryt herfur und howt Im In sinen halsz.

149. Der hatt wöllen den schilt oben hinyn wünden. – Den schilt solt Man ynen Sehen und der stich geschrenck solt Sin gescheen.

150. Hie hon ich versetzt mit macht und bin beliben ston und hon mynen starcken stich getan. – Als der sinen schilt Ingeschlagen hat und wolt den worlousz machen und den schilt hon von Im geschlagen das ist Im gebrochen.

VII.   Schild

151.   So ist der fur dretten und nempt In by dem halsz und wurfft In mit dem Schilt. – Als der den schilt In geschlagen hatt.

152.   Da Ist das stuck volbracht wie vor geschriben statt.

153.   Der hatt In gebunden zwischen den Schilt und den man und hatt Im den hacken geslagen umb sinen fusz und wyl Ryssen. – Darumb er mir ist komen zwüschen mich und den schilt Des ich billich engült.

154.   Von dem anbinden So mag man unden und oben Ryssen zu baiden syten.

155.   Es ist aim als dem andern und oder oben wie er des komen mag. – Aber usz dem obern anbund oder bochen So mag ain yeder dem anndern griffen In sinen schilt und von Im Rysen ob er mag.

156.   Usz dem Infallen und griffen wie vor geschriben statt welicher denn nit wöll lon so mag es wol an ain Ringen gon.

157.   Nun Merck das stuck recht als Nun der hatt wollen schlahen und So ist er vast gestanden und latt die Rechten hand vom Schilt und gryfft dem In den Elbogen und stosst In von Im das er sich verkertt. – Hie hatt er dem den Schilt Ingeslagen und hinterbunden.

158.   Als der den gestossen by dem Elbogen hatt als vor geschriben statt. – So kert sich der gar umb und stoszt den Schilt In den und ist stuck und bruch bolbracht zum end.

159.   In dem anlouffen So hat er In hinder Tretten und bracht In In die höin und fürcht er werd geworffen. – Das ist aver ain starcker anlouff und, usz dem anlouff So hatt er In hinderbunden und wirt In werffen oder er mus wörlousz werden.

160.   Hie hatt er In bracht zum fall wie vor geschriben statt. Und macht aver ain end mit dem fryen stosz.

161.   Hie stond sie bayd zu dem verkerten anbund Inn zuslahen und ain annder Nöten.

162.   Doch so wyl der geben die schweche In die sterckin och sin arbait daby merckt. – In dem bochen so bend yeglicher den andern gern losz und das er Im kem hinder den Schilt und machte In wörlouss.

163.   Hie hatt er die schwechin volbracht In die sterckin und mag

stossen oder Rysen. – Da hett der die sterckin verlorn und wirt nyder geryssen.

164. Hie ist das stuck wolbracht wie vor geschriben statt zum end.

VIII. Gekehlte und Hacken-Schilde

165. Nun lant sich der Nöten und gatt unden In die schwech und Nempt Im den fusz und Ryszt. – Aber usz dem anbinden und ainander Nöten So hat er den oben übertrungen.

166. Das sind die zwen fryen Notstend dar usz man suchen mag und finden allen vortail und Innlouffen und werlousz machen und vil hüpscher arbait die man darusz machen mag so man sust dehain wer hatt denn den schilt. – Ich wartt des ends.

167. Und hatt Im der das treffen gezuckt und Im oben In den Schilt gestochen. Wurd mir der schlag an sin halsz. – Hie hatt wöllen der anbinden und bochen. – Ker umb so vindestu das Stuck volbracht.

168. Hie würt das stuck volbracht als vor geschriben Statt.

169. Da hatt das schiltfechten ain end – das unsz gott allen kumer wend.

IX. Degen (Dolch)

170. Hie vacht an der Tegen, gott der wöll unser aller pflegen. – Der hatt gestochen von dach. – Der hatt versetzt mit ainer hand und hatt den Tegen von im gewarnt. – Der wyl obnen Nyder Stechen. – So gatt der unden uff mit versatzung und syls im Brechen.

171. Der ober schilt für den Stich. – Der Stich fry von Tach. – So macht der den undern Schilt mit ain stossz. – Der Sticht unden zu dem.

172. Für den obern stich so würff din lincken arm uff und fach sin Stich uff den lincken arm und macht mit dinem Tegen stechen oder slahen. – Als Ich hon gestochen, So ist es mir gebrochen. – Aver für den obern Stich würff den linken Arm für und mit dem Tegen umb sin arm und würff In von dir. – Der hatt sin stich volbracht und des bruchs nit gedacht.

173. Als der ober Inn hat gestochen So hatt der Es mit dem lincken arm

gebrochen und grifft Im mit dem Tegen zwischen die bain und
zuckt In uff und würfft in von Im. – Als der oben hinyn hatt
gestochen So hatt er mit dem rechten Arm versetzt und wint den
Tegen umb sinen arm und tryt damit für und würfft in von Im.

174. Da ist der uszgangen und der bruch über das fahenn. – Als der
In beschlossen hatt. – So hatt der In beschlossen mit der schär. –
Der hatt gestochen oben Inn.

175. Für den obern stich Ain grosser worff gang mit dem rechten
Arm uff und fal mit dem lincken arm uber sinen rechten arm
und würff In von dir. – Da Ist das stuck und wurff volbracht.

176. Als der obnen Nyder hatt gestochen so ist er uff gangen mit dem
rechten arm und grifft Im mit dem lincken Hand In sin Elbogen
und Truckt In von Im so kert sich der gar umb und würfft In
über Rucken. – Hie ist volbracht stuck und bruch zwinach.

177. Für den obern stich hatt er sinen rechten Arm uff geworffen und
sinem Stich hinweg geholffen und ersticht In. – Der hatt
gestochen und Ist Im der stich gebrochen. – Das sol sin ain
vahen usz der schäre den arm oder den hals.

178. Aber für den oben stich ain armbruch und fas sin stich uff den
lincken arm und griff mit der Rechten hand under sinen arm
und zuck an dich. – Aber für den obern stich fach sin stich uff
din Rechten Arm und Tryt für und schlah Imi din lincken arm
an sin halsz und würff In uber die huffen.

179. Aber für den obern stich würff den Rechten Arm uff und fach
sin stich daruff und gryff mit der lincken hand In sin Elbogen
und truck In von dir für sich Nyder. – Der bruch ker dich gar
umb und würff In über die huffen.

180. Für den undern stich so schlah mit der rechten funst In sin arm
und stosz din Tegen In In. – Hie hatt einer als gutt als der ander.

181. Aber für den undern stich schlagh mit diner rechten hand Sin
stich hinweg und Slah In mit der lincken hand an sinen hals und
Tryt mit für und würff In von dir. – Für den undern stich fach
sin stich In din bayd hend und wirf Im Sin arm uff die lincken
Achsel und brich In ab.

182. Hie ist der armbruch vie vor geschriben stat. – Aber ain fryer
stand mit dem schilt für den obern stich oder für den undern.

183. Als der den schilt hat gemacht. – So hatt der den obern stich

verwent und Stotzt den tegen mit dem hefft zwäschen sinen arm über den schilt und würft In von Im. – Da Verbringt er dasselb Stuck.

184. Der hatt den gefangen usz der schäre. – Der bringt dem die Schäre. – So hatt och der den beschlossen mit der schäre umb den hals. – So macht der den Bruch und wirt In werffen.

185. Hie ist er uffgangen mit dem Schilt für den obern stich. – So hatt der den stich erlogen und slecht unden uff und sticht. – Der hatt aber den obern Schilt gemacht. – So hat der aber den Stich erlogen und ubergryfft Im bayd Arm und tut In werffen.

186. Der hatt den äbich angebunden und wyl In übergryffen. – Der hatt gestochen Oben hinyn. – Hie hatt er In übergryffen und den beschlusz volbracht. – Als der gestochen hatt.

187. Hie hat er versetzt mit der schär und mag In hinweg Stossen mit welicher hand er wyl. – Der hatt sin stich volbracht. – Der statt in der fryen hutt. – So halt sich der Im zwiffelstich und hat den Tegen uff dem Rucken und mag stechen mit welicher hand er wyl.

188. So hatt der versetzt mit sinem lincken arm und hatt In oben übergryffen und hatt Im under Sinem schenckel undergryffen und wirt In werffen. – Der hatt gestochen oben Inn mit macht und ain fryen Stich volfürt. – Der maister hatt sich über senhen und ist bayde ain stuck.

189. Als der mich überloffen hat mit aim fryen stich oben Nyder. So hab ich den lincken arm uff geworffen und versetzt und mit mym rechten Arm hab ich In umb sin hals gefaszt und wirg In Nider. – Hie hatt er In Nyder gewirckt und macht ain end.

X. Ringen

190. Der anfall usz den Armen zu ringen. – So hatt der versetzt mit dem lincken Arm und Sticht och von Tach. – Als der gestochen hatt von Tach.

191. Die habent birlichs gefasst ain Arm unden den anndern oben und ligend In dem streb. – In dem Streb So schlefft er sin hopt durch sin Arm und zuckt In uff.

192. Als der gefaszt hatt usz den Armen. – So stoszt der mit sinem

Rechten Elbogen uff sinen Rechten arm und mit dem stosz So gryfft er Im under sinen rechten fusz und zuckt In uff und wirfft In über ussz. – Der hatt es nit gutt. – Der wyl den werffen uber den schenckel.

193. Hie wyl der den bringen In Trapen ob er Im möcht Brechen den Arm. – Hie hatt der Im den arm Bracht uff die achsel und wöllen Im den abbrechen.

194. Usz dem Fasen so würfft er In uber den Schenckel. – Hie hatt er In hinder Tretten und Stosst In über den schenckel.

195. Aber ain glichs Byrlichs Fasen. – Uss dem Byrlichs fasen So zuckt Er den undern Arm und ergryfft In by dem hopt und Swenckt In von Im.

196. In dem Fasen So wyl der durchgon. – Hie Ist er Im durchgangen und würfft In über den Rucken.

197. In dem durchgon So ist das der Bruch und wirckt In by dem halsz. – Aver ain Bruch uver das durch gon In dem durchgon So zuck den fusz hindersich und ergryff In by dem halsz.

198. Das Hecklin Fürsich. – Das Hecklin der Bruch mit dem Schlag.

199. Wen ainer ain ergryfft hinderwertligen So wartt ob dir möcht Sin schenckel werden und züch In her durch und Richt dich uff. – Aber so ainr ain faszt hinderwertz so Tryt mit dinem fusz hinder sich zwüschen Sine bain und gryff im nach dem schenckel.

200. Das ist ain heben hinderwertz der Bruch darüber Nem In by dem har und züch In über die achsel. – Das haiszt ain beschulsz wyl er den ledig werden So brich Im die finger oder Buck sich und werff In uber Rücken.

201. Wen ainr ain ergryfft und bayd arm unden hatt und dich uff zucken wyl So gryff Im mit bayden Henden In sin Antlit und schüb In von dir so latt er dich. – Der latt sich mit wylen Faszen und er mag In dennocht nit von Im werffen er würfft In.

202. Der wirfft den mit dem halben hecklin und usz dem halben hufft Ringen. – Hie hatt er in geworffen usz derselben Arbaitt.

203. Ain ober huff Ringen. – Uber das oberhuff Ringen so Sucht er ain Bruch.

204. In dem Ringen So hatt er Im hinder Tretten und In über den Fus ... – In dem streben so wyl der dem den Fus unden usz Slahen.

205. In dem Ringen hatt er In uffzuckt und lofft mit Im umb das

haiszt ain Schwindelringen. – Der hatt den gefaszt mit bayden henden by dem halsz und erschütt In so stoszt der In von Im.

206. Ain verkert Ringen Ist Aver Swer zu heben. – Ain Ringen usz dem Tegen mit dem arm wirgen von Im kern.

207. Das haiszt ain Buben Ringen. – Der bruch darüber Fall Im mit dem knü In sin macht.

208. Der hatt den gefangen und fürt In by dem arm. – Hie latt er sich fürn und gatt gern und In den gon so zuckt er In uff und würfft in hinder sich an Rucken.

209. Der hatt wöllen durch gon. So hatt er Im zuckt und ergryfft In und truckt In Nyder. – Das haiszt ein Achsel Ringen und kumpt von dem halsz fassen.

210. Usz dem fassen So Tryt der dem den Schenckel ab. – Wen dich ainr Nötten wyl In dem Ringen und fast hept So heb mit Im und In dem heben So gib dich In die Schwechin und heng Im hach so wirt er dir In ain schlossz.

211. Der hat den by dem goller gefaszt und Schlecht Im unden den fus usz. – Usz der vorigen argait So würfft Er In über die undere huffen.

212. Am arm winden ob er In möcht bringen zwüschen die Bain. – Hie hatt er das vor geschryben Stuck volbracht.

213. Der hatt den gebracht In den Trappen. – In dem zucken schlecht er In an sinen halsz und würfft In über die huffen.

214. Der bruch über das Fassen. So Tryt mit dinem fus hinder sich zwüschen sine bain und würff In über die Siten ab. – Der hatt den gefasst by bayden Armen uff dem Rucken.

215. Aber ain Fasen by dem halsz. So gryfft er Im In die Elbogen und tryt für und stoszt In über den schenckel. – Ain hindertretten und mit dem lincken Arm In sinen halsz und stosz den über den Schenckel.

216. Da hatt der den In dem hecklin Recht. – Der Bruch über das hecklin. Im gryff als er das hecklin schutzt so nem das ober huff Ringen So ist das hecklin Brochen.

217. Das ist ain uszbindiger bruch uber das Hecklin und über das ober huff Ringen. – Das ist och ain bruch übers hecklin oder huff.

218. Da hatt der den bruch volbracht uber das hecklin. – Der hatt

wollen louffen In das hecklin oder In die obern huff So went sich
der und macht den bruch.

219.   Usz dem halszfaszen so macht der ain schlosz. – Hie hatt er In
beschlossen und würfft In über die schenckel.

220.   Hie hatt er In über gryffen und würfft In über die under hufft
Ringen In ain schlosz. – Als sie glich gefaszt haben So stoszt er
mit sinem Elbogen In sinen rechten Arm und übersch ützt und
felt Im umb sinen schenckel und würfft In.

221.   Hie ist der wurff volbracht wie hernach geschriben stat. – Aber
ein Bruch über das hecklin wen es dir das hecklin schlecht So fal
Im In die kniekellen mit dem knü.

XI.   Messer

223.   Hie Facht an das Messer. – Gott wöll unnsr nit vergessen. –
Der wyl howen von Tach. – So wyl der Im den how versetzen
mit macht.

224.   Der hat sin how volbracht. – Der hatt den schlag versetzt und
wyl In übergryffen.

225.   Hie hatt er In übergryffen und howt In durch den kopff und hat
das vor geshriben Stuck ain end.

226.   Der howt Fry von dach. – Der hatt versetzt mit gewenter hand
und wyl für tretten und Ryssen.

227.   Hie hatt er für getretten und Ryszt mit dem messer. Des stosz zu
der Elbogen sol man nit vergessen.

228.   Der hatt den angeloffen In Zorn und hatt In wöllen howen durch
den kopff. – So hatt der versetzt unden uff mit macht und In
sinem uffzichen hat er Im sin hand abgehowen.

229.   Hie Tryt er für und Slecht In gar Nider zu tod.

230.   So hatt der Im versetzt und hatt In über gryffen mit dem Arm und
stoszt messer In In. – Der hatt gehowen von Tach uff den man.

XII.   Messer und kleiner Schild (bouclier)

231.   Das sind die Zwen fryen Stend mit dem buckeller und mit
dem Messer.

232.   Hie hatt der versetzt mit dem Buckeller und Messer. Des

übergryffens sol er nit vergessen. – Der hatt gehowen dem In
sin versatzung.

233. Als der uff mich hatt gehowen So hab ich Im versetzt und usz
der versatzung übergryffen und how Im durch den kopff.

234. Da hatt der Im versetzt und Stoszt In von Im und Ryszt mit
dem Messer.

235. Als er In von Im gestossen hatt So volendet er das stuck und
Stoszt das schwert durch in.

236. Aber howt der von Tach. – Hie hatt der versetzt fry und loufft
Im daby Inn.

237. Hie Ist Im der Ingeloffen und hat das Swert durch In gestochen.

238. Der Statt für den Stich. – Der Wyl In stechen.

239. Als der gestochen hatt So hott Im der In Sinen Arm der ober
how ist och gutt für.

XIII. Einer gegen zwei

240. Das Ist der Notstand wen zwen über ain Sind. – Hie wyl ich
uff In howen. – Da versetzt der mit Eppicher hand und wirt sich
wenden und howen zu dem hindn. – Hie wyl der och howen. –
Da versetzt er mit dem tegen und buckeller.

241. Im wenden so howt er In durch den kopff So fellten der hinder
an So beschlüszt er In och.

XIV. Kämpfe zwischen Mann und Frau

242. Da Statt Wie Man und Frowen mit ainander kempffen
söllen und stand hie In dem anfanng. – Da statt die frow
fry und wyl schlagen und hatt ain stain In dem Sleer
wigt vier oder finf pfund. – So statt er In der gruben bis
an die waichin und ist der kolb als lang als Ir der Schleer
von der hand.

243. Hie hatt Sie ain schlag volbracht. – Nun hat er den schlag
versetzt und gefangen und wyl Sie zu Im ziehen und nötten.

244. Da hatt er sie zu Im gezogen und under sich geworffen und
wyl sie würgen.

245. Da hatt sie sich usz Im gebrochen und understatt Sie In zu wirgen.

246.   Hie hatt sie In gebracht an den Rucken und wyl In wirgen und
        ziehen usz der grub.

247.   Da hatt er sie zu Im gezuckt und würfft sie In die gruben.

248.   Als sie schlahen wyl So ist sie Im zu nach Tretten das er sie
        ergryfft by dem schenckel und wirt sie fellen.

249.   So schlecht er sie Für die brust. – Da hatt sie Im den schlöer
        umb den hals geschlagen und wyl In würgen.

250.   Da hatt sie In gefaszt by dem halsz und by sinem zug und wyl In
        usz der gruben ziehen.

XV.   Schwertkämpfe zu Ross

251.   Usz dem über Illen So wyl der versetzen mit dem Stich. – Der
        Sprengt In an und wyl In über Illen.

252.   So hatt der versetzt mit epicher hand und wüst für. – Als der
        gehowen hatt.

253.   Hie ist das stuck volbracht und hatt In gehowen In den schenckel.

254.   In dem anrenen So facht der sinen how und wint Im Sin Swert
        In Sin antlit. – Der hat gehowen.

255.   Hie hat er den schlag versetzt und über felt Im und ryszt das
        Swert von Im.

256.   Das schwert Nemen underougen.

257.   Das Swert Nemen hinderwertz.

258.   Als der hatt gehowen. – hatt der Epich versetzt und Ist Im
        überfalen umb den halsz.

259.   Hie versetzt der Fry und wyl den überfalen. – Der hat gehowen
        vom Tach.

260.   Hie ist er Im Ingefallen und das vorgeschriben Stuck
        volbracht.

XVI.   Ringkämpfe zu Ross

261.   Das Ringen zu Rossz. – Hie hatt der In beschlossen und uber
        gyryffen underougen.

262.   Der bruch uber Das vorgeschriben Schlosz hatt Im gezuckt Sin
        übergryffen und In by dem halsz ...

263.   Da würfft der Rossz und Man.

264. Das übergryffen und der beschlusz hinder sich. – Der hatt den hinderwertz ergryffen.

XVII. Kämpfe zu Ross mit Spiess und Schwert

265. Der Entwert dem den Spiesz mit dem Schwertt.
266. Hie Ist das stuck volbracht als vorgeschriben statt.

XVIII. Kämpfe zu Ross mit Armbrust gegen

267. Die Illenden. – Wie sich ainer halten sol in der flucht mit dem armprost.
268. Der wyl den under das pfert Renen. – Hie hatt der den geschossen und stoszt Im den Spiesz mit dem Armbrost hinweg und würt In ergryffen by dem halsz.
269. Hie wyl der den Recht empfahen mit dem Spiesz. – Wie sich ainer halten sol mit dem Spiesz gegen ainem mit ainem Armbrost.
270. Hie ist das vor geschriben Stuck mit dem Armbrost und Spiesz volbracht und hatt In ergryffen by dem halsz. – Das buch hatt angeben hans talhoffer und gestanden zu Mallen.

BIBLIOGRAPHY

Amberger, J. Christoph, *The Secret History of the Sword*. Baltimore, MD, Hammerterz Verlag, 1996.

Anglo, Sydney, *The Martial Arts of Renaissance Europe*. London and New Haven, Yale, 2000.

Baldick, Robert, *The Duel: A History of Duelling*. London, Chapman and Hall, 1965; New York, Clarkson N. Potter, 1965, and Barnes and Noble, 1996.

Brown, Terry, *English Martial Arts*. Hockwold-cum-Wilton, Anglo-Saxon Books, 1997.

Canby, Courtland, *A History of Weaponry*. New York, Hawthorne Books, 1963.

Castle, Egerton, *Schools and Masters of Fence*. London, George Bell and Sons, 1885, revised 1892, and (revised) Arms and Armour Press, 1969.

Clements, John, *Medieval Swordsmanship: Illustrated Methods and Techniques*. Boulder, CO, Paladin Press, 1998.

Cole, Michael D. (ed), *Swords & Hilt Weapons*. London, Multimedia Books, 1989.

Döbringer, Hanko, *Fechtbuch* (1389). Nuremberg, German National Museum, Codex Ms. 3227a.

Du Boulay, F.R.H., *Germany in the Later Middle Ages*. New York, St. Martin's Press, 1983.

Dürer, Albrecht, *Fechtbuch* (1512), in Friedrich Dörnhöffer, *Jahrbuch der Kunsthistorischen Sammlungen des Allerhöchsten Kaiserhauses*, XXVII. Wien, F. Tempsky, 1910; Leipzig, G. Freytag, 1910.

Edge, David and John Miles, *Arms and Armor of the Medieval Knight*. New York, Crescent Books, 1988.

Hergsell, Gustav, *Die Fechtkunst im XV und XVI Jahrhunderte* (The Art of Fighting in the 15th and 16th Centuries). Leipzig, K.W. Hiersemann, 1896.

Hergsell, Gustav, *Talhoffers Fechtbuch aus dem Jahre 1467*. Prague, 1887.

Hooper, Nicholas and Matthew Bennett (eds), *The Cambridge Illustrated Atlas: Warfare: The Middle Ages, 768–1487*. Cambridge and New York, Cambridge University Press, 1996.

Hutton, Alfred, *The Sword and the Centuries*. London, Grant Richards, 1901; New York, Barnes and Noble, 1995.

Keen, Maurice (ed), *Medieval Warfare: A History*. Oxford University Press, 1999; New York, Getty Center for Education in the Arts, 1999.

Meyer, Joachim, *Grundtliche beschreibung der freyen ritterlichen und adelichen kunst des fechtens* (A Thorough Description of the Free, Knightly and Noble Art of Fencing). Strasbourg, 1570.

Novati, Francesco, *Flos Duellatorum il Fior di Battaglia di Maestro Fiore Dei Liberi* (Flos Duellatorum, The Flower of Battle, by Master Fiore Dei Liberi). Bergamo, 1902.

Oakeshott, Ewart, *Records of the Medieval Sword*. Woodbridge, Boydell & Brewer, 1981.

Oakeshott, Ewart, *The Sword in the Age of Chivalry*. London, Lutterworth Press, 1964; Woodbridge, Boydell & Brewer, 1994.

Oman, C.W.C., *A History of the Art of War in the Middle Ages*, 2 vols. London, Methuen, 1924, and Greenhill, 1991.

Rapisardi, Giovani, *Fiore Dei Liberi's Flos Duellatorium*. Padua, Gladitoria Press, 1998.

Ringeck, Sigmund, *Fechtbuch* (*c*1440). Dresden, State Library of Saxony, Ms. Dresd. C 487.

Steinmetz, Andrew, *The Romance of Duelling in all Times and Countries*. London, 1868, reprinted, Richmond Publishing, 1971.

Talhoffer, Hans, *Fechtbuch aus dem Jahre 1443* (Gotha Codex). Gotha, Research Library at Schloss Friedenstein, Ms. Chart. A 558.

Tower Fechtbuch I.33 (*c*1280). London, British Museum, Ms. No. 14 E iii, No. 20, D. vi.

Wise, Arthur, *Art and History of Personal Combat*. Greenwich, CT, Arma Press, 1972.

ACKNOWLEDGEMENTS

I would like to thank the following people for contributing to the production of this book through their guidance, generosity and patience: J. Mark Bertrand, Jörg Bellinghausen, John Clements, David Cvet, Stefan Dieke, Terry Doughman, James FitzGerald, S. Matthew Galas, Esq., Steve Hick, Pete Kautz, Jared Kirby, Norbert Krines, Mike May, Greg Mele, Kelly Parker, Dr. Patri Pugliese, Tim Ruzicki, Jill Sultz, Melissa Tucker, and especially Lionel Leventhal and Kate Ryle of Greenhill Books.

Mark Rector
2000